Acknowledgements

In my partner, Kent, I have the greatest gift a woman could receive from God. I often joke that God loves me more because He gave me Kent. Thank you, my husband, for the unconditional love, support and understanding that has always been the very foundation of our relationship.

To my precious sons; Josh, I have often credited you with saving my life because had you not been born I would have gone in an entirely different direction. Your patience, quick wit and unwavering love have been mainstays for me. You are my friend as well as my son. Caleb, you are my bold, strong and sweet-spirited boy. Your imagination has inspired me over and over again. I love you both dearly and cherish your uniqueness.

To my dear friend Teri Schafer who labored over this manuscript, helping through the many changes. Teri, I couldn't have done it without you.

To Sheila, Ruth and Elizabeth for all your efforts and contributions.

To Sheryl and Bill, thank you for all the ideas and helping complete this project.

To Lisa Bevere, your advice and keen insight were much appreciated. Thank you for helping to tie up the loose ends.

To all my family and friends whose faithfulness, encouragement and support for this project never wavered.

To Daddy, thank you for believing in me.

Most importantly, thank You, heavenly Father. Without You there would be no book and I give You all the glory for every word written. Without You, I am nothing.

Table of Contents

I Could Not Call Him FATHER

Beverly Mattox

Whitaker House

Unless otherwise indicated, all Scripture quotations are taken from the *King James Version* (KJV) of the Bible.

I COULD NOT CALL HIM FATHER

Beverly Mattox
P.O. Box 940782
Maitland, FL 32794-0782

ISBN: 0-88368-505-1
Printed in the United States of America
Copyright © 1997 by Beverly Mattox

Whitaker House
30 Hunt Valley Circle
New Kensington, PA 15068

Library of Congress Cataloging-in-Publication Data

Mattox, Beverly, 1956–
    I could not call him Father / Beverly Mattox.
        p.   cm.
    ISBN 0-88368-505-1 (trade paper : alk. paper)
    1. Mattox, Beverly, 1956–   . 2. Christian biography—United States.
3. Fathers and daughters—United States.   I. Title.
BR1725.M3554A3 1997
277.3'082'092—dc21
[B]   97-21548

1 2 3 4 5 6 7 8 9 10 11 12 / 06 05 04 03 02 01 00 99 98 97

Foreword

A child's relationship with his natural father can provide a beautiful example of the loving, intimate relationship we can experience with our heavenly Father. The eternal and unconditional love of our heavenly Father is available to all.

When the nurturing years of a child's life are compromised, the potential father-child experience is thwarted. This can affect us indefinitely in many ways, both in the natural and in the spiritual realms.

I Could Not Call Him Father presents the story of a daughter who was bound by years of hurt and disappointment. This led to unforgiveness toward her father because of his years of violence, alcohol abuse, persecution and even murder. But the miracle of God's glorious and unconditional love transcended the bitterness and unforgiveness, and brought healing. Because of that healing, this daughter can say the words "I love you, Daddy" from a heart overflowing with love.

This inspired book has a message for this generation. *I Could Not Call Him Father* is a book which will help bring liberty to those bound by bitterness and unforgiveness. It's pages clearly depict God's ability to reach a heart hardened by the hurt of the past, and transform it to one filled with love and compassion.

Benny Hinn
Pastor/Evangelist
Benny Hinn Media Ministries
Orlando, Florida

Beverly has written a beautiful story of love and forgiveness and what happens to the human spirit when both are present. She has also shown the effects of bitterness, anger, and unforgiveness.

Then she gave us the scripture to prove that God loves us even when we rebel and keep unforgiveness in our hearts.

She shows us how her health was affected by her unforgiving spirit and the change that came physically and emotionally when God helped her to forgive.

Oral, my husband, says that as Christians we must have a testimony and it must be shared with those to whom we minister. We must show others that God is no respecter of persons. What He did for us He will do for them.

Beverly has a wonderful testimony. I believe all who read it will be blessed and examine their hearts to see if any unforgiveness exists. Thank you, Beverly, for this true experience you have shared.

Evelyn Roberts
Speaker/Teacher
Oral Roberts University
Tulsa, Oklahoma

Beverly Mattox offers a thought-provoking journey into what salvation has to offer to a broken heart and a broken life. This compelling book is one you can't put down as you walk with Beverly through one discovery of God's provision to another.

What I found most paramount, as a thread running through each chapter, was how forgiveness and God's blessing go hand-in-hand, and how essential that we realize it and walk in it.

I highly recommend this honest and captivating story of one woman's courageous road to freedom. I *Could Not Call Him*

Father can benefit every believer and be used as a powerful tool to the unbeliever as well.

Beverly sends a clear message to humanity that there is hope for everyone and every situation through Jesus Christ. I believe anyone who reads her account will never be the same.

Ellen Parsley
Speaker/Teacher
World Harvest Church
Columbus, Ohio

This is a love story—not just of Bev and Kent, but of the Savior who rescued Bev from unforgiveness and turned her family toward God. This is a book of hope and healing. I know Bev's desire in telling her story is that others will know God's love and share in His redemptive plan.

Also, it will be a book that can be given to someone not yet a Christian and they will be able to see how if given to Him, God can take a mess of circumstances and build a house of glory!

Connie Haus
Speaker/Writer
Hostess of the "Coast to Coast" television program
Concord, California

I Could Not Call Him Father is a journey from turmoil to triumph. Read it and you'll experience a God that's real and a Father that's true!

Lisa Bevere
Speaker and Author of "Out of Control and Loving It"
Apopka, Florida

Introduction

"I must speak that I may find relief."
Job 32:20

For years I tried to pretend my past never happened. Plagued by the painful memories of my childhood, I had become a survivor and learned to deal with life the way it was dealt to me. But one day I made a most amazing discovery. I discovered the joy of salvation and that old things pass away when you become a new creation in Christ Jesus.

Like so many others I have the dubious distinction of being born during the birth explosion that occurred between 1946 and 1964. Roughly one-third of our population today make up the post-World War II baby-boom generation. The confusion and lack of direction that many of us experienced during the sixties and seventies is still affecting our lives today. There are so many people that are still living day-to-day, not realizing that God has an eternal plan for their lives and that God's power to save increases as your power to understand His gift of salvation increases. God's love and miracle-working power are limitless and available to all. Our response to His extended love is the only limiting factor. God's power to save is not limited—nor is His desire to save. The Bible states in Revelation 22:17 that "whosoever will may come." He is waiting for your heart-felt cry to call upon Him.

This book is for God's glory and that is why I am able to

write it now. My desire is for others to experience freedom from the hurts and wounds of their past just as I have. If in telling this story just one person comes to know the Lord Jesus as Savior and experiences deliverance from the pain of their past, enabling them to forgive, it will be worth it.

It is my prayer that as you read this book, God will touch you and you will receive healing in your heart. Writing this book has been part of my healing process, and I thank my heavenly Father for always being there for me even when I did not reach out to Him.

A Child

If a child lives with criticism he learns to condemn
If a child lives with hostility he learns to fight
If a child lives with fear he learns to be apprehensive
If a child lives with pity he learns to feel sorry for himself
If a child lives with jealousy he learns to hate
If a child lives with encouragement he learns to be confident
If a child lives with praise he learns to be appreciative
If a child lives with approval he learns to like himself
If a child lives with recognition he learns to have a goal
If a child lives with fairness he learns justice
If a child lives with friendliness
He learns that the world is a nice place in which to live

Author Unknown

CHAPTER ONE

The Road to Nowhere

But you, O God, do see trouble and grief;
you consider it to take it in hand.
The victim commits himself to you;
you are the helper of the fatherless.
Psalm 10:14

One...two...three...four. I counted slowly as each of the huge steel prison doors slammed shut behind me. One by one they closed and as they did the sound was so loud...so piercing. My body spontaneously jerked in response each time the loud clang rang out. It bounced off the walls of the corridor and echoed all around me.

I held my son's hand tightly as I continued to walk down the hallway. Caleb, my little buddy...I was so glad he was there. And following close behind was my husband, Kent. I didn't look back at him or speak a word as we walked methodically toward the exit. I was filled with so much emotion about what had just happened, and I needed time to sort it out.

As I walked out of the dark prison and stepped into the warm sunlight, a feeling of relief swept over me. Although I had entered the prison just three hours before, it now seemed like years ago. So much had happened in those three hours. Visiting a prison had seemed so foreign to me, so unnatural, not to mention the reason for the visit. I was there to visit inmate #1013428 who was serving twenty-eight years to life for murder—my father whom I had not seen in 16 years.

We arrived at our car and I put Caleb in the back seat. As Kent started the car and began to drive away, my mind was filled with thoughts of the last three hours. In the background, I could hear my son's voice. He was asking questions faster than Kent could answer them.

Immersed in thought, I continued to reflect on everything that had just occurred inside the cold prison walls. The image of an older, gray-haired man walking toward me in the visitors' room kept playing over and over in my mind. The feelings of intimidation and fear hadn't been there this time when I looked into his drawn face. In fact, the emotions that welled up within me were very different this time. I actually felt compassion for him.

As we continued to drive away from the prison, I thought about all the times as a child that I had been consumed with fear as I looked up into the harsh face of my father. A tall man, he always seemed to tower over me which added to the intimidation I felt. But today a most unusual thing had occurred when I saw him. The fear and intimidation which was once there had been replaced with a deep sense of compassion. Could it be possible that after all these years of hurt and separation, I was actually feeling love?

I felt so different at that moment, different from anything I could remember in my past. The fear, anger, hurt, rejection and every other fragile, wounded emotion which had been a weight too heavy to bear had vanished. At that moment I felt almost weightless and free, much like a bird must feel after being released from a cage. It was as if I was floating along, being carried up into a beautiful clear-blue sky, lifted by a gentle summer breeze. Up, up, away from anything that could threaten or intimidate me. I felt free...liberated...as if I had been freed from my own prison.

Through all the thoughts that flooded my mind, I heard my husband's tender voice say, "Are you okay, Bev?" His voice drew me back through the long tunnel of thought. As I turned to answer him, attempting to set aside all my reflections of the past hours, I realized I was crying.

"Yes, I'm all right," I responded, reaching for a tissue to wipe away the tears. As I blotted the tears from my face, I realized I didn't feel unhappy or sad. These were not tears of sorrow or anguish, they were tears of joy and freedom. Although I had just walked out of the physical prison to which my father was confined, I felt as if I had just taken the first step out of an even greater prison. A prison stronger and more impenetrable than institutions made of bars of steel. This was an emotional prison that had held me captive for twenty-three years.

As I look back on my past, I now realize that the happiest and most glorious day of my life was the day I came to the end of myself and invited Jesus Christ to be the Lord and Savior of my life. But before I made the amazing discovery that I was truly a sinner and needed the Lord Jesus to rescue me from my road to self destruction, my perspective on happiness was quite different.

I'll never forget April 11, 1971. I was fourteen years old and I was part of the live-in, love-in, make-love-not-war, burn-your-draft-card, burn-your-bra mindset. I had spent the whole day getting very high at a "party house" near my home. On this day I wasn't doing anything but smoking pot (marijuana).

In the midst of this party atmosphere, my boyfriend came into the room and told me that something was going on at my house. He said there were cops everywhere. His voice was serious as he spoke but I wasn't overly concerned. This wasn't the first time cops had been at our house. Maybe my father was beating my mother again. He had done it so many times I had lost count. Or perhaps he was drunk again. It could be any number of things. A neighbor must have called them again. My father was a mean, angry man and was often in trouble. What could it be this time?

As I thought about the possibilities of what might be happening at home, I leisurely smoked one more joint. Then I got myself together and made my way home.

I was greeted by my mother as I walked in the front door. Without saying a word, she handed me an official-looking piece of paper. I opened the paper and began to read it. In the background I could hear my grandmother crying softly.

The State of North Carolina vs. the defendant...the undersigned, C. H. Davis, on information and belief, being duly sworn, complains and says that at and in the county named above and on or about the 10th day of April, 1971, the defendant did unlawfully, willfully, and feloniously and of his malice aforethought kill and murder. (This statement was taken from the original arrest warrant.)

A warrant for murder! He had been arrested for a murder-for-hire scheme. I knew my father was a lot of things, but a murderer? I had been afraid of my father for years, but in the last three years our relationship had deteriorated to the point that I was in total rebellion.

I glanced over my shoulder at my mother. She was just standing there, staring into space, speechless. My grandmother was still sobbing in the living room.

Although there was so much grief and sadness all around me at that moment, I didn't shed a tear. In fact, I felt as if I had just been pardoned and was now free...almost happy. It seemed that my father had finally gotten into a situation that no one could get him out of. And now he couldn't hurt my mother or me or my sisters. Maybe it was finally over.

At the time of my father's arrest, I was fourteen years old and had been smoking pot for a year. I did LSD every weekend and was well on my way to drugs like heroin and cocaine.

During the months following my father's arrest, life was one big party for me. I stayed high and was oblivious to what my mother was going through. I partied continually and became more and more rebellious.

My early memories in life contain loving times with my mother, Sunday School, church activities, and many of the things that are a normal part of a child's life. My sisters and I spent most of our time with our mother. My father wasn't home much when we were there. If he did happen to be at home in the daytime, we knew we had to be very quiet.

The early memories that stand out in my mind concerning my father were the times when we did manage to do something that brought us to his attention. For example, the time we were taken to the movie and left there. When no one came to pick us up, we walked across to the other theater and watched that movie, too. Afterward, there still was no one there, so we walked the few short blocks to my grandfather's house. When my father found us there, he took us out into the front yard, put me and my two sisters across the fender of his car and beat us with his belt in front of the whole neighborhood. No one tried to stop him or even question his reason for doing this even though our ages ranged from only two to six years at the time. This was just one of many incidents during my growing up years that caused fear to be a dominant force in my life.

We were not the target of his anger most of the time, my mother was. I used to think that the alcohol was the reason for his bad temper. But unfortunately, he didn't have to be drinking to be mean. So many people deal with an alcoholic parent or parents today, but in our small community, my family was the only one I knew of that everything that happened was so glaringly public. By the time of his arrest for murder, he had a rap sheet a mile long. It was reported in the newspaper each time he had to appear in court or each time the police had to answer a call for domestic violence in our home.

By May of that year my mother was fed up with me. She couldn't handle me anymore. I thought I knew what I wanted in life and I was going to get it. The more I drifted away from my mother, the more time I spent with my boyfriend.

The last week of school something very traumatic happened. My boyfriend and I had a fight and he left in anger. Determined to find him, I left the house and started walking down the road to look for him. A car stopped to offer me a ride. Because I thought it was a boy from school and I was desperate to find my boyfriend, I got in. But as soon as we started to drive away, I knew I had made a mistake. Before the ride was over, the man tried to rape me. I jumped from the car and ran down the road screaming. Two girls heard my screams and stopped to pick me up. They took me to the police station. Because I had gotten the license number of the man, the police were able to quickly pick him up. He had quite a record and eventually served two years in prison because of the incident.

When my mother found out what happened, she was beside

herself. This, on top of everything else was too much for her. She had experienced all she could handle. We had a fight and I left home the next day.

At fourteen years of age, I had nowhere to go so I moved in with an older girlfriend. I was already sexually active and because there was no parental supervision, it wasn't long before I found out that I was pregnant by my boyfriend. Armed with a fake birth certificate, he drove me to Washington, DC for a legal abortion.

The next year, I met my son Josh's father. Because of my fathers' imprisonment and the circumstances that my mother had been left to deal with, we rushed in to an early marriage. I married him at seventeen and six months later I became pregnant with Josh. The marriage lasted legally for six years, but we actually separated when my son was two years old. We divorced when I was twenty-three years old.

By the time I was twenty-one, I had already had one abortion, been married, given birth to a beautiful baby boy and been separated. Now I was a single parent trying to find my way in the world. Unfortunately, I fell right into another relationship and before I was twenty-two, had yet another abortion.

I learned early in life to be a survivor. Because of how volatile my father's temper was, we did anything we could to keep that anger from exploding. We ran, we hid, we were quiet, we tried to be good but nothing could guarantee us refuge from an unexpected explosion of anger.

That's how my journey on "the road to nowhere" began. I can remember feeling terrified of my father when I was only five years old. This terror soon turned into bitterness and unforgiveness. Such unforgiveness gripped me that I was in bondage to it. It would take me years to overcome all the circumstances that led to this bondage.

It wasn't until I came to know Jesus Christ as my Lord and Savior that I realized how bound I really was.

When we deserve God's love least is
when we need it most.

Walk With Me

It hurts me Lord, to feel this pain
Knowing I will never be the same.
Make me stronger through this all
For I have stumbled, now I fall.

———

Lift me up to know your love
I lift my face to you above
Walk with me down this road
Help me carry this heavy load.

———

Learning every step I go
Your love and wisdom is all I know
I was blind, but now I see
That only you Lord, can save me.

Trisha Phelps

CHAPTER TWO

The First Step to Freedom

For I know the thoughts that I think toward
you, says the Lord, thoughts of peace and
not of evil, to give you a future and a hope.
Jeremiah 29:11

Carteret County in North Carolina has to be one of the most beautiful places in the world. The county is surrounded by water. The Atlantic Ocean is to the south and the Intracoastal Waterway is to the north. I grew up in Morehead City, North Carolina, and I am a Carolina girl through and through. The area will always be very precious to me because all my family is still there and it was home for many years.

We have made our home in Orlando, Florida for the past eight years, but it was in Atlantic Beach, North Carolina that I met my husband, Kent. We actually met in 1983, but it wasn't until the summer of 1984 that we spent any time together. I was still in college and working part-time as a bartender in a private night club. He came in on occasion but we hadn't gotten to know one another. As a single parent I didn't have a lot of time to hang out in bars. My top priority was to be the best mother to Josh that I could be and to become educated.

The first time Kent and I had the opportunity to have a conversation was an unusual circumstance in itself because I was on summer break from school and had gone to this club for the first time as a patron instead of an employee. As he reintroduced himself it seemed like the whole evening had been orchestrated so I would be in this exact place at this exact time. We talked for hours and made plans for the next day.

I met him at the resort he was staying in and we headed to Beaufort, which is right across the bridge from Morehead. I love this little fishing village because it has been totally restored and is very beautiful. On this particular day we had planned to have lunch together and I wanted everything to go just right. After all, it was our first date. As we headed out I was very excited because it was an absolutely gorgeous day. There were beautiful white fluffy clouds in the Carolina blue sky and as we came down Front Street all the sailboats were lined up and seemed to be saluting us. There were people milling about and a really festive feeling in the air. I took him to the Dock House for lunch and we had the best time. I'm sure I fell in love with him that very first lunch. The sun was hot and the waterfront breeze was cool as we got to know one another that afternoon. Hours passed and afternoon turned into early evening. Neither of us wanted the day to end so we made plans for dinner as we walked through town.

We had been drinking beer and smoking pot for most of the day and were in high spirits to say the least. We decided to have seafood so we went to the Net House and there we switched to drinking wine. We were still having the best time and as we sat talking. I looked at him, wineglass in hand, and said, "You know, you are going to be a preacher someday." I was shocked! That was the very last thing on my mind, I can tell you! He was just as shocked as I was, probably more so! He said, "Who are you?!" I was very embarrassed. After I blurted that out I became completely sober. I didn't try to explain why I said that, I just tried to act like it had never happened and so did he. The whole atmosphere around us changed and we both felt self-conscious. Our lives were forever changed in that moment. Little did we both know how God was about to fulfill a vision He had given me two years earlier.

During the years of 1982 and 1983 I had a drug route which I ran regularly. On these drug runs I never did any drugs whatsoever. I was always clearheaded and alert. Fifteen years ago it was nothing for me to get in my car and drive three hundred miles, do the deal and drive back. Most of my driving was done between midnight and dawn. One particular night I was driving back home with eight ounces of cocaine in the car. Even then that was enough cocaine to put you in jail for a very long time. I was alone and about eighty miles from home.

At this point in my life God could not have been further from my mind. I was totally immersed in the drug culture and loved all of its benefits. So you may be able to imagine how surprised I was to be driving along on a dark road when all of a sudden the sky opened up in front of me as though I had pulled into a drive-in theater.

I saw myself standing beside a tall, black-haired man and we both had microphones in our hands. We were standing on a platform and there were people as far as the eye could see. It was so real and I knew, not in my intellectual mind but in my spirit, God was showing me a vision. I said aloud, "God, you have the wrong woman."

I heard an audible chuckle. Not from the outside but from

the inside. A chuckle! Many people may not believe God has a sense of humor but I am here to tell you He does! He tells us in His Word that laughter doeth good like a medicine so the Creator Himself must enjoy a good chuckle on occasion. I believe He did that night. I promptly forgot the whole thing and went about my life as though it had never happened.

Now, two years later, that same vision of this tall, dark-haired, intoxicated man who I said would someday become a preacher came back to me. I had no idea why I had said he would be a preacher one day and I certainly had no idea the affect it would have on my future husband.

My background as a Baptist had introduced me to salvation, but I didn't know a thing about the gifts of the Spirit or anything beyond being saved. Kent, on the other hand, had been raised in a Pentecostal church and had at an early age made a real and true commitment to Jesus Christ. He, too, had made the decision that the Lord would have to wait while he enjoyed what the world had to offer.

We lived in different cities so our relationship developed long distance. Because of my association with drugs it didn't take long for me to realize how much of Kent's life revolved around either getting drugs or doing them. His life was filled with making money and spending it. We always had a good time when we were together, but I didn't think we had any kind of future together.

During the two years we spent dating we had many ups and downs and I watched as he became more and more dependent on marijuana and cocaine. There would be nights he would get so high he couldn't sleep and he'd ask me, "Do you think it's time yet?" I knew exactly what he was talking about. Even though we never talked about him becoming a preacher it was always there between us. Each time he would ask I would tell him that was between him and God.

When I finally reached the point I couldn't take the kind of lifestyle we were involved in any longer, I told him I loved him but it was time for us to part ways. He promised things would change and asked me to marry him. I wasn't foolish enough to believe he could change overnight, but I was hoping for the best. We were married on June 14, 1984. By mid-summer he was using cocaine more heavily than he ever had.

We were thousands of dollars in debt and he was frantically trying all kinds of drug-selling scams to make money quick to cover his debts. The hole just kept getting deeper and deeper.On August 28, 1984 I rushed him to the hospital as he overdosed on cocaine. That would be the first of many trips to the hospital. Over the next few months he overdosed three more times.

In early September he resigned his position as project director for the company he had been with for four years. He took a job in Virginia Beach, Virginia and we packed up and left. We had no money and the position salary of $70,000 annually was left for a commissioned position that on his best week there he made $35. As Kent tells it, he went from hero to zero overnight. I was working but we had the bills of a $70,000 per year income. Kent's car payment alone was $633 per month. In short, we were in a mess.

Kent's health was a wreck. I look back at photos of him during that time and it breaks my heart to see how pale and sickly he was. Kent's parents came to see us for Christmas that year and they took one look at their son and knew he was ill. They didn't know what was wrong, just that he looked really bad.

We drove to Williamsburg, Virginia and tried to have a good time. Everything was so beautiful for the holidays but we didn't enjoy any of it. On the way home Kent collapsed and we took him directly to the hospital. He was diagnosed with hypoglycemia and told to go home and rest.

Kent's mom and dad took immediate action. A bag was packed and they put him directly into the car. They drove him straight to Alabama and put him in the hospital. My son Josh and I packed up the townhouse and waited for my two brothers-in-law to come pick us up.

For Josh it was his third move in eight months. Before we would be settled again he would attend schools in three different states that school year. The doubts I had about marrying Kent resurfaced and seeds of bitter resentment were beginning to sprout. Even though my life had always had an element of crisis they had been my mistakes to work out and Josh had always been protected. He had led a relatively stable life living in a city close to all his family, but because I was now married he was being uprooted and moved all over the Eastern Seaboard. It didn't help matters that Kent had left us behind in two different cities.

In the meanwhile, Kent had been told by the family doctor he was suffering from extreme stress and his body was worn out from the drugs. He needed time to recuperate and rest. Going back to work right away was out of the question. We were now all in the same house living with Kent's sister, her husband, their three children, his mom, dad, Kent, Josh and myself. I had not lived with parents since I was fourteen years old. Kent's dad, Tom, who is the patriarch of the family was in charge of everything. They were in the process of selling their family home and their stay with their daughter was temporary as well, but for the two and a half months we were all under the same roof we all had to make a lot of adjustments, especially Kent's nieces. I know it was really hard for them to give up their privacy, but it was the first thing to go.

We had been married eight months but it felt more like eight years. We had no money, no home and we were so far in the woods that they all still joke that they couldn't get Saturday Night Live until Tuesday. At the time I didn't think that was very funny. I've come to appreciate that joke over time. It didn't take me long to realize that in some ways his family felt I was at least partially responsible for Kent's breakdown. Everyone was kind to me but there was an undercurrent of suspicion that if he hadn't married me none of this would be happening. That was very hard to deal with because once again I was being rejected. Those seeds were sprouting bitter weeds.

Kent started carrying around a little New Testament Bible. At first I didn't pay much attention to it. He also started attending church. He didn't say too much about what he was up to until the night he came in crying and told me he had been saved. He told me all about how his heart was pounding in his chest to the point he really thought he was going to die. He began to pray the young man preaching would stop so he could give his life to the Lord because he knew if he died right then he would go to hell. Right in the middle of the service the preacher did stop preaching and he went right over to Kent and said, "Young man, you need to get right with the Lord!" Kent broke right then and there and invited the Lord Jesus to come into his heart.

I am here to tell you I was not thrilled. We were still penniless, homeless and now as far as I could tell my precious husband was becoming a religious fanatic. I couldn't take much more! But there was more! Much, much more! The next Sunday Kent made arrangements for him and Josh to be baptized. I figured he wanted Josh there for support so we went ahead with the baptismal. At the time I had never been in a Pentecostal church so I wasn't sure what to expect. You have to understand I hadn't spent a lot of time in church for the past two decades.

The baptism was really beautiful and I cried as I watched my husband and my son. It was an emotional reaction and the feeling didn't last. Once the service was over, so was the reaction. What I didn't realize was the Holy Spirit had already begun to work in my spirit. Kent was praying over and over, "God save Bev, God save Bev!" Had I known, I probably would have run for my life!

In the pressure-cooker atmosphere we were living in it only stands to reason that tempers would flair and before long they did. I had been on my own for sixteen years and had made my own decisions and choices. For the first time in my adult life someone else was in control of even the smallest details, including what food we would eat. I wanted out of the situation in a big way.

On the night I finally exploded it was the lack of privacy that got to me. I left the house that Wednesday night to clear my mind and decide what I was going to do. When we arrived in Alabama we still had some pot left but I had smoked almost all of it. There were a few roaches (marijuana cigarette butts) in the ashtray of our car. As I dug around in the ashes I heard a gentle voice ask, "What are you doing digging around in that filth?" I knew it was the voice of God but I was determined not to respond. I backed the car out of the drive, lit the joint and inhaled deeply.

Just as the pot started to relax me God spoke again only this time there was only one way to respond. As I drove down that dark country road, tears of frustration turned to tears of joy as the Lord spoke clearly to me saying, "Now is the time, come unto Me my child." Wave after wave of pure love poured over every inch of my body. I began to weep uncontrollably and right there in the front seat of my car I gave my life to Jesus Christ. I had taken the first step toward freedom! After a while, when I could drive, I went back to the house and told Kent what had happened to me and that's when he told me how he had been praying for me.

A month later we went to Orlando, Florida and through a

former employee of Kent's we learned of Pastor Benny Hinn's church and began to attend services there the day after we arrived. On March 9, 1987 we made a public confession of our faith at Orlando Christian Center.

Many years later Dr. Oral Roberts would ask me how I found the Lord and I told him very sincerely that I didn't find Him— He found me.

Where there is faith, there is peace.

The Voiceless Cry

Jesus, hear us, and let our cry come unto Thee.
That voiceless cry, that comes from anguished hearts,
Is heard above all the music of Heaven.
It is not the arguments of theologians that solve the problems
Of a questioning heart,
But the cry of that heart to Me,
And the certainty that I have heard.

Author Unknown

CHAPTER THREE

Painful Memories

For You, Lord, are good, and ready
to forgive, And abundant in mercy
to all those who call upon You.
Psalm 86:5

The day is the 11th of April, the year is 1995. I am back at the beach visiting my in-laws and as usual we are having a great time. For many years I have dreaded this time of year because it is the anniversary of my father's imprisonment. The year 1995 marks the twenty-fourth year he has spent behind prison walls. I begin counting the days down as soon as April arrives. This year is no exception but for some reason I really almost forgot it today.

Because of the sixteen years that I was estranged from my father this was a day of mourning. All of the emotions that never were allowed to emerge would battle their way to the surface of my conscious mind and I would relive Easter Sunday of 1971 over and over again.

That day will forever be etched in my memory not just because my father was arrested, but because I literally entered into my own prison, complete with spiritual guards of rejection, abandonment, fear, bitterness, hatred, and unforgiveness. Over the next twenty-three years I was as bound as my father was.

I did not want to forgive him. The shame of having a parent in prison is bad enough but strangely, I was more understanding of how he came to that end than I was of his literal abandonment of his family before he ever went to prison. He would disappear for days on end, leaving my mother with little or no money. He would appear just as suddenly as he had left in a bad mood and spoiling for a fight.

My own bitterness stems from what I perceived as a young child as his rejection of his family and total lack of commitment to take responsibility for us. There was always somewhere else that was far more important for him to be than at home.

The ultimate lack of concern hit home for me when I came to accept a betrayal that occurred when I was only seven years old. For a very short time my mother worked outside of the home. After an act of domestic violence she had left my father and was legally separated from him. They reconciled and we moved into a different home but they kept the same babysitter. I looked up to this girl because she was a senior in high school and because she really took a lot of time with me.

Looking back, I realize I was starved for attention and she was willing to give it. The sad thing is it was perverted attention. It took years for me to really understand that her behavior was inappropriate and I had been molested. My sisters remember to this day how she would hold me in her arms and kiss and fondle me. As heartwrenching as that is I know my dad was at home sleeping on at least one of these occasions.

I have never told him of these incidents but in my heart I felt betrayed by his lack of action to protect me. I was only seven years old and felt as though there was no one to turn to. From that time on my distrust grew in his ability to protect any of us.

By the time I was eleven years old, I completely distrusted his every action. Low self-esteem became a monkey on my back that I hid with a rebellious attitude and a very smart mouth. It was all too obvious I was never going to be able to please this stranger who was my father. He made it clear I was too stupid, too ugly, too smart-mouthed to ever do anything right.

All of these emotions held me captive, preventing me from walking in liberty. I never seemed able to win my natural father's approval so I knew beyond a shadow of a doubt I would never make much of an impression on God. How could He possibly find anything lovable about me if all my natural father could see was my awkwardness and my unloveliness? I sought other sources to fill the void my father had left and a never-ending cycle started. The more I sought fulfillment, the less I found. I was left with a bigger void and on top of that was guilt.

As time marched on I tried unsuccessfully to have a relationship with my natural father but after seven years I just gave up. While we struggled to hold on to him as a father figure he just wanted our help to get him out of prison. During that seven-year time span many things occurred that just were not conducive to a good relationship between the two of us.

After many attempts of trying to continue our father-daughter relationship, the futility of trying to have any kind of relationship with him began to wear me down. I could not meet his demands. The prison element added a dimension of unreality to a situation that was already hard enough to comprehend. Our entire visits were spent with him making more and more outrageous demands. The pressure was tremendous. He wanted to get out of prison and we, his children, were his only access to the establishment that imprisoned him.

The final blow for me was when he introduced my sister to a bank robber and asked her to dig up his stolen money. She did go to the area it was supposed to be hidden. There was no money there. The bank robber then broke out of prison. He was picked up at the bus station two miles from my mother's home. He had two things with him, a loaded gun and my mother's address. My mother hid at my house for three days. I realized then that I could not continue to live like that. I finally stopped going to see him.

My mother died several years later of ovarian cancer. For years I told people both my parents were dead. As a matter of fact, Kent did not know about my father for the first year and a half we were together. We were saved in the third year of our relationship and from the very beginning Kent encouraged me to make contact with my father. I just could not do it. All the fear, anger, resentment, bitterness, rejection and unforgiveness would just boil inside of me.

Finally, after I had been saved for about three years I wrote to my father and he wrote back. By this time I had come to an understanding about spiritual battles and with my husband urging me on I continued to write to him.

I wish so much I could tell you these were loving letters full of the goodness and mercy of the Lord, but quite the opposite is true. All of the hurts and bitterness flowed from my poison pen. Everything I had ever done or said that I thought would hurt him I threw in. I wanted him to know every drug

I had ever taken, every sexual encounter I had ever had, how I aborted two of his grandchildren and why it was not going to work for us to be in each other's lives.

In Joyce Meyers' book, *Beauty for Ashes*, she says, "One of the main truths the Lord spoke to me while dealing with the forgiveness issue was this: hurting people hurt people!" I wanted to be full of God's love but I was just beginning to realize how much I myself was hurting. I had given him our phone number and he called one time and asked for money to help get him a lawyer. I promptly changed my number and tried to forget he existed. My relationship with my heavenly Father was in the same shape. I couldn't get past my unforgiveness to reach out to Him.

At approximately the same time, I made the decision not to forgive my father, we were in the midst of a tremendous struggle to pay an IRS debt and my husband had just become a pastor. With my background I felt less than qualified to be a pastor's wife but I was giving it my best shot. I was involved in everything in our church and was ministering more and more especially after Kent started traveling each month.

I felt the Lord wanted me to share about my past experiences and my story of salvation. I thought, no problem. So I gave a moving oratory of my glossy version of all that I just shared with you. I got the distinct impression my heavenly Father was not happy with the gloss. Yet still I persisted in sharing the cleaned up version each time I had the opportunity to share my testimony.

I wanted to know God's Word so I studied every day. I went by a daily Bible study so imagine my surprise when every time I opened by Bible it fell open to Matthew 25:41. Are you familiar with this part of scripture? Let me refresh your memory. Verse 41 says, "Then He will also say to those on the left hand, 'Depart from Me, ye cursed, into everlasting fire, prepared for the devil and his angels'. Verse 42 through 46 goes on to tell us, "For I was an hungered, and ye gave Me no meat; I was thirsty and you gave Me no drink; I was a stranger, and ye took Me not in; naked, and ye clothed Me not; sick, and in prison, and ye visited Me not. Then shall they also answer Him, saying, Lord, when saw we Thee an hungered or a thirst, or a stranger, or naked or sick, or in prison and did not minister to Thee? Then shall He answer them, saying, Verily I say unto you, Inasmuch as ye did it not to one of the least of these, ye did it not to Me. And these shall go away into everlasting punishment; but the righteous into life eternal."

You would think I would have gotten the message but I did not want to forgive my father. I could not forgive myself and I refused to tell the whole truth about my past. If I could have seen what the next two years of my life were going to be like I would have made an entirely different decision. For the next twenty-four months I battled tremendous depression and anxiety. Everything and every relationship I was involved in began to fall apart. But, as you will soon see, God wanted me to know He is the God of forgiveness and I could accomplish nothing without His blessing.

I went about my merry hard-hearted way living a Christian life the best way I knew how, doing all the right things and saying the right things but it wasn't all working out the way the Bible kept telling me it should. The first area we noticed not meshing with the Word was our financial situation. The Lord was blessing us but there never seemed to be enough money. Secondly, my relationships all fell apart. Thirdly, my health began to deteriorate. I was diagnosed with stress related diverticulitis and my colon totally shut down. My abdomen began to swell and I gained 30 pounds of waste. The years of holding onto bitterness had finally manifested in my physical body. My body was poisoning itself and I finally got to the point I couldn't do anything but lie in bed.

Around this same time I decided to write my father again and he wrote me back and wanted to know what kind of Christian was I that I could turn my back on a man in prison? Matthew 25:41 started playing over and over in my mind. I began to ask myself the same exact question, "What kind of Christian am I?" At that time I was a sick one! Proverbs 28:14 says "Happy is the man who is always reverent, but he who hardens his heart will fall into calamity."

You see, I was no longer ignorant of God's principles, yet I had chosen to continue to live in unforgiveness! Calamity was knocking at my door. I had heard a teaching about a link between arthritis and bitterness and the Lord reminded me of it. As I put the sickness of my body together with the sickness of my spirit I began to realize that I was left with no choice but to get on my face before God and confess my sins.

In Psalm 6:2 David cries out "O Lord heal me, for my bones are troubled." Bones are mentioned throughout the Psalms as a symbol of health for the whole body. By the time this revelation occurred to me my whole body ached and I literally felt as though I had been run over by a truck! I had been carrying this load for so long that every area of my life was being affected. God designed us so every organ in our body would line up with the Word of God and work in perfection. When our emotions are holding us captive it affects the entire rest of our body.

Unforgiveness may not always be the cause of a sickness but if, like me, you have chosen to hold on to that bitterness you could very possibly be making yourself sick.

Let me encourage you now to ask yourself if there is an area you just can't seem to let go of. If you answer yes to any of these questions you can be free. Release it and let healing begin.

1. Is there a hurt you can't get beyond?

2. Are you harboring a negative attitude toward anyone?

3. When you think about certain situations does it make your stomach churn and your head hurt?

I can't give you a three-point formula that will bring deliverance and healing but I can share with you how God began to bring healing into my life. If there are unresolved issues in your life that come as a result of verbal, physical or sexual abuse you most likely have created your own defense mechanisms to protect yourself and have built walls to keep you in. The saying that the walls you build to keep others out also serve to keep you in, is very accurate. There is no way to become the person God intended you to be if you have such high walls around you that no one can get in and you can't get out.

Every individual has issues to deal with. It's how we choose to deal with them that either sets us free or keeps us bound. Once we come to the understanding that the abuse is a physical manifestation of spiritual problems we can begin to understand that our past does not have to control our future.

It took me years to look beyond my father's behavior to try and discover why he had turned into the man he had. To look past someone's actions and find out what shapes them into the person they have become can be one of the first steps to healing.

I have more compassion now for my natural father than ever before. One of the keys to being able to forgive him was coming to understand the overwhelming emotions he must have experienced when his own father was killed. Trying to understand him as a person has often been difficult. These things were never mentioned until this year, when my father finally spoke of the death of his father.

I never knew my grandfather so all of my knowledge of the

relationship between father and son has come from different family members. Before my paternal grandfather was killed, from what I understand, he ran his home like a naval base. There was tremendous discipline and guidance in my father's life until he was sixteen years old and his own father was taken from him. I can only speculate how the death of my grandfather affected and shaped him.

My grandfather died at the hand of a former employee over a financial dispute. In a drunken rage he shot my grandfather squarely in the chest with a double-barrel shotgun. His death radically changed the course of my father's life just as my father's imprisonment changed mine. Little bits and pieces of how his life was affected have given me insight into him as a person.

If you are so wounded that you can't let go of the hurt, start out by asking the Lord to give you the desire to be free. That may seem like a little thing but continue asking Him until you feel He has truly given you the desire to be free. There are no time limits so don't feel that you have to accomplish it in any set amount of time.

When I knew beyond a shadow of a doubt that I would write this book, I cried out to God and begged Him to let me share my story some other way. I just couldn't believe that I had anything to say that could really help any one else. There were so many times, that I thought I had made it to point B and I was actually stuck on point A. I struggled and fell so many times yet each time I did my heavenly Father was right there with open arms encouraging me to try again, reminding me He was proud of my efforts and He would be with me every step of the way. Remember, He is not concerned with perfection, but with progress!

Take the first steps toward healing and freedom and let Him do the rest. Every day ask Him to help you walk in forgiveness. Every day release the individual that has hurt you to the Lord. Very simply put, tell the Lord, "Lord, I choose to forgive _____ *(fill in the person's name)*. I can't do it on my own but with Your help I can walk in forgiveness today." The most important choice is to be obedient to God. 1 Peter 5:7 says "...casting all your care upon Him; for He careth for you." In the New Century Version Translation of the Bible, Isaiah 41:10 tells us, "So don't worry because I am with you. Don't be afraid, because I am your God. I will make you strong and help you." You have His word. He will make you strong and help you.

Until I came to the understanding that only I could make the choice to be obedient to God's Word I stayed bound. It was only by confessing my sin to Him that I was able to begin the healing process. As Christians we are able to confess our sins to a loving Father because of His grace. But there are a lot of folks that aren't sure exactly why we have to confess our sins and are even more confused as to how to go about it. 1 John 1:9 tells us, "If we confess our sins, He is faithful and just to forgive us our sins, and to cleanse us from all unrighteousness." Colossians 2:13-14 explains, "When you were dead in your transgressions...He made you alive together with Him, having forgiven us all our transgressions."

I came to the understanding that all God wanted from me was to admit I was wrong and I was trying to do things in my own strength with little or no regard for the plan He had. He desires our honesty so we can experience His healing power of forgiveness. He wants to be reconciled with us without the burden of our guilt. Once we confess our sin freely to Him then our fellowship can continue in accordance with His plan, not ours.

My relationship with my father was slowly developing via the mail. Sometimes he was kinder than others, but I started looking for his letters in the mail instead of dreading them.

His letters all had one theme, if you want to know me better, come see me! This line of communication went on for two years.

Finally, it was curiosity that got the better of me. I made the decision to make the trip and planned it so it would coincide with a baby shower for my sister, Glennie. Kent took the time off to join me. In my heart I wasn't expecting much from him or from myself and frankly I felt as though I was doing God this big favor by being obedient. The trip was on but I really wasn't turning back flips with excitement. As the time drew nearer and nearer all of my fears showed up to hurl accusations.

The conversations went like this. Fear yelled out, "Remember the times all he had to do was look at you to reduce you to tears?" Anger said, "How about the time you got your new bike and he wouldn't let you ride it until you had your picture made with it? To make you stand still he pinched you so hard you cried. In the picture today all you remember is the hurt you felt instead of the joy of riding the bike." Rejection wouldn't be outdone so he threw in, "Think of all the times you waited to tell him something you were happy about and when he finally did show up he wasn't the least bit interested in you." Bitterness kicked in and adds his two cents worth, "Why should you go see him, what has he ever done for you?" But unforgiveness was the worst. You see, the spirit of unforgiveness had held me captive for so long it really thought all it had to do was remind of how badly my mother had been treated, so he said, "You know, if he had treated your momma better she would still be alive today!" This was usually unforgiveness' ace in the hole.

This time I was prepared for that attack because the Lord had been so faithful to remind me of how my mother continued to pray for my father and she always encouraged all of us children to remember that no matter what he had done,

41

he would always be our father. So instead of giving in, my resolve was strengthened to see this through.

God will not give up on you.

And the Lord,
He it is that doth
Go before thee;
He will be with thee
He will not fail thee,
Neither forsake thee:
Fear not
Neither be dismayed.

Deuteronomy 31:8

CHAPTER FOUR

Memories of Yesterday

The fruit of righteousness is sown in peace
of them that make peace.
James 3:18

The bright lights of the auditorium are focused on the platform. It is the second night of the crusade in Anaheim, California. The auditorium is packed. Faith, hope and rejoicing are almost tangible as healing after healing is reported. Watching from the congregation I rejoice with them and wait expectantly as a young mother makes her way up the aisle and onto the platform. She has two small children crowding around her legs and they are all weeping tears of joy.

As she begins to share her testimony of months of chemotherapy and endless doctor's reports telling her there is nothing else that can be done for her medically, my mind starts to play over and over the same scenario being played out several years ago when it was my mother being told that same heartbreaking news.

Like this young mother, my own mother's faith was strong and she believed with all her heart she too would receive healing from the ovarian cancer that would eventually take her life. As my thoughts raced back over time, the same question began to take over my thoughts. It isn't the question, "Why wasn't my mother healed?" No, I have had nothing but peace about her dying, because I know she walked right out of that sick and diseased body into heaven. Even though I was not saved at the time I knew she had experienced enough here on earth and Jesus was taking her home.

The question that weighed so heavily on my mind was, "Why wasn't I a better daughter to her when I had the chance?" On the platform two little girls are weeping before God and this assembly of twenty thousand people, confessing their belief in the healing power of the blood and how they have prayed and prayed for their mommy to be healed.

While I listened I thought back to being in the hospital room listening to my mom as she spoke of her own childhood and what her dreams and hopes had been. The most important thing to her was knowing that she had been a good mother to her five children. She told me many times over the six months that we stayed in the hospital all she had ever wanted to be was a good wife to her husband and a good mother to her children. Even though I reassured her that she had in fact been a wonderful wife and mother she didn't seem to have peace about the job she had done in raising us. I think she knew even then she was dying and there had been no fruit from her prayers for us.

As she shared her own story of what she expected from life she spoke of not having her mother to learn from, and how hard it had been knowing her mother made the choice to not be a part of her life. It had remained shrouded in mystery.

Even though I had heard bits and pieces over the years about my maternal grandmother's disappearance when my mother was about seven I still had many unanswered questions.

My grandmother took her children to a movie and told them to walk home. Three days later my grandfather received a call that his children had been abandoned in an apartment building. The kids were hungry and needed a place to go. My mom and my uncle received one birthday card each after she left and that was the last anyone ever heard from her. My grandfather raised my mother and my uncle. They lived in my great-grandmother's home until they both married.

As a small child I spent many happy hours in that very home. There was no lack of love and it wasn't until I became a rebellious teenager that I ever questioned my mother's ability to reach out to me or teach me.

Marriage certainly had not provided the haven she craved and needed. The sense of rejection and abandonment she carried over the years must have grown to enormous proportions by the time my father went to prison. To my knowledge, the two of them never discussed her mother's disappearance or my grandfather's murder.

I have asked my father if they ever supported one another's feelings about these two key issues but he said they didn't talk too much about either incident. It is doubtful I will ever know exactly what either parent experienced or felt. My mother has been in heaven for many years and my father is not a man given to sharing his private emotions. The one person and the effects of these events that I do know something about is me and how I have battled to survive.

I was twenty-six years old when mom died. She was forty-six. My father had been in prison for ten years and she had worked very hard, going to college full time and holding down sometimes two and three jobs to support us.

I left home at fourteen partially because I was rebellious and wild but also because I couldn't stand the pressure of living at home. Looking back over the decisions I made then is why I am sitting in the middle of a glorious healing service questioning myself about being a good daughter.

During all of those years I could have been such a blessing to my mother and family, I wasn't. I did what pleased me. Guilt is the demonic attack that tries over and over to steal my joy. Isaiah 32:17 says, "...And the work of righteousness shall be peace; and the effect of righteousness quietness and assurance forever." James 3:18 tells me, "...And the fruit of righteousness is sown in peace of them that make peace." Making peace with ourselves is sometimes an almost impossible task. Purging ourselves of the burden of guilt is the ultimate act of self-forgiveness.

When we are able to freely accept the forgiveness extended to us by Christ dying on the cross, we are then liberated from the burdens that have weighed so heavily on us. Even though it is difficult, if we truly desire reconciliation with those we have harmed or those who have harmed us, it is possible if we are willing to do whatever it takes, regardless of the cost. Until there is the sacrifice of forgiveness, true healing cannot begin toward others or for ourselves.

In many ways I am still working toward the goal. For years I couldn't accept the responsibility of the choices I had made. Even now I am a far cry from being righteous but if the fruit of righteousness is sown in peace of them that make peace and the work of righteousness is peace, then as I continue to allow the Holy Spirit to work in me I will expect the effect of righteousness to be quietness and assurance forever! Forgiveness is the seed I have sown into my relationship with my natural father. Peace is the fruit I am expecting from my heavenly Father.

This time as my mind is drawn back to the present I feel a real sense of freedom. Guilt has held me captive long enough. The anointing does break the yoke of bondage. As I stand to my feet giving God the glory for the woman's miraculous healing I know that He who has begun a good work in me will complete it. Forgiving myself is the first step toward true healing and I've taken that step.

Our greatest need next to Jesus Christ
is inner peace.

Don't you realize you can choose your own master?
You can choose sin (with death) or else obedience
(with acquittal).
For the wages of sin is death,
But the free gift of God is eternal life through
Jesus Christ our Lord.

Romans 6:16-23

CHAPTER FIVE

Entrepreneur of the 80's

*Father, I have sinned against
heaven, and before thee.
Luke 15:18*

Until the time my mother was hospitalized I had always held a job, sometimes two or three part-time positions that allowed me the freedom to run the covert drug operation that was my main source of income. During the six months I spent at the hospital with her I was unable to work so there was no cover for the money that was coming in to me. I don't know if I had been under surveillance before the winter of 1983 but the increased drug dealing activity without a legitimate job cover left me wide open for an investigation. As the illness took it's toll on my mother's health I continued to pay the bills with no apparent means of support.

In June of 1983 the radiation treatments were over and from all reports my mother was cancer free. She was sent home to recuperate and I immediately left for a two-week vacation in New York. My son Josh had been staying with his natural father and was looking forward to a two-week stay at a Christian summer camp in the beautiful North Carolina mountains.

At the end of the two weeks we returned home to discover my mother was very ill and would have to be hospitalized again. It was a very frustrating time for all the family because we wanted the cancer to be gone. The doctor told us she was fine but needed a few more tests and some rest. Two weeks later she had gone to be with the Lord. The cancer had moved into her lymph glands and there was nothing the doctors could do.

We were so unprepared for her death that when the call came from my aunt she said, "Beverly, your mom has gone," I actually asked, "Where has she gone? She's too sick to go anywhere!" The next few days went by in a stark contrast of unbelief and reality. All of the preparations for the funeral had to be made and decisions about my youngest sister Liz and little brother Brant's living arrangements had to be sorted out. Liz came to live with me and Brant went to live with our uncle. It was an unbearable situation but we did as my mother's will asked.

During all of this the Lord kept reminding me I needed to be in church. There were several reasons I felt I could not go to church so every time I felt the urging of the Lord (I didn't know it was the Holy Spirit knocking on my heart's door), I would remind Him I was a drug dealer, I hadn't been in church in years, plus where would I go?

Everyone in town knew my past, my father's past and the church I had grown up in had requested we remove our name from the church roster because my mother believed in all of the gifts of the Spirit, including healing and speaking in tongues.

At the time I didn't even know what that meant. As far as I could tell it meant we weren't welcome in the church we had grown up in and don't call us and we won't call you. So each time I felt the pull to be in church I hardened my heart just a little more. Rejection from peers in the world is hard to overcome, but rejection from your church family can be devastating. It took many years to overcome the concept that God Himself had rejected me and asked me to leave His house. I felt completely justified in telling Him no, thank You, but I'm not interested in going to church.

My lifestyle continued in much the same way it had before my mother's illness and death. I went back into the bar business and continued to freelance and cater events. I was more involved in the drug business than I had ever been before.

In the small community I lived in everyone knew everyone and for the most part there were always small deals going on mostly for personal use not profit. My main interest was the profit. I wasn't interested in doing drugs and I really believed I was providing a service that was needed. I didn't know any drug addicts, just people who liked to party on Wednesday nights and weekends. It was all very socially acceptable and also very illegal.

In the winter months there were very few tourists in town so all of the locals partied together and it was rare that an outside person would be included in house parties or local get-togethers. There was a sense of security and well being since there were usually only people around that you had known for years. Personally, I didn't attend a lot of parties because I didn't have time for it and I was very careful about who knew my business. I knew a lot of people because I worked in a bar, but I was very selective about who came to my home unless I was hosting a party of my own. Then everyone came because it was not business, just fun.

In the Spring of 1984 we had several parties that were open house. I lived right on the beach so it was the ideal place to welcome spring and to have a good time. I had been dating the same man for three years and our relationship was changing because of a job transfer for him. I was trying to figure out how we could end this relationship gracefully. While we were both trying to work through this change we stayed in quite a lot.

As we were watching TV one night there was a knock on the door. I recognized the man as a new fellow in town who came to the bar I worked in and had come to a few of the parties we had during the spring. He asked if he could come in and watch TV with us and we said sure, come on in. During the course of the evening we smoked a joint and when the movie ended he asked me if he could buy a bag of pot from me. I told him I didn't have any pot for sale but I could give him a couple of joints. He offered to pay for them but I told him no, I didn't sell pot, I just smoked it.

Now watch how faithful the Lord is to protect one of His own. Even though I had repeatedly turned my back on the small, still voice urging me to return to the house of the Lord, He prepared me for what was about to happen. This was the second truly supernatural experience God allowed me to have before I was ever born again. Remember the vision God gave to me in the car?

As the time drew closer for my friend to make his move I still had mixed feelings. As I sat one day in my room brushing my hair I was considering how both our lives would change. I was sitting at the vanity watching my reflection in the mirror when I heard from within, what was a voice that sounded very much like my own mother saying, "Beverly Joy, you've got a lot of sense!" I sat right up and turned to look around the room. I cried out, "Martha?" (that is my mother's name) then I said, "Martha!" again. After I cried out I heard, "Here you are sitting worrying about some man when you are getting ready to go to jail!" I stopped brushing my hair and stood up saying, "My

God, My God! That man I gave the pot to is an undercover agent!" I felt as though I had been warned that my lifestyle choices were all about to come crashing down around me.

I immediately got dressed and went to a local restaurant to see the girl who had been dating this man. I asked her point blank if he was an undercover agent. I also told her if she did not know she had better find out because if he was a lot of people would be going to jail. Her best friend was listening to our conversation and went home and locked herself in the house and waited to be arrested. She had sold him two and a half ounces of cocaine.

The girl he had been dating went home and asked him if he was an undercover policeman. He told her no. He left town that night to go to Raleigh to get his warrants in order. On Mother's Day, 1984, I woke up to two State Bureau of Investigations officers knocking on my bedroom door. I was disoriented at first and asked them if there had been an accident and if my family was okay. They said everything was okay with my family but I was being arrested for giving marijuana to an undercover agent. I asked what he meant and he told me even though I didn't sell any pot, the amount in question weighed more than a quarter ounce so it was considered to be a large enough amount of a controlled substance to merit my arrest.

The whole arrest was televised and before it was over thirty-two people had been arrested for selling some form of illegal drug to that one undercover agent. Out of the thirty-two people arrested that day I was the only one not to serve prison time. The only reason I was arrested at all was because of the seeds in the pot weighing so much. They had been watching me for a long time and it was worth it just for the bust.

Yes, God did protect me from going to jail that morning but the irony of this miracle is not that I didn't sell the undercover agent the pot, but that the warning from the Lord gave me the time to clean up my act and remove anything that would have sent me to jail when my house was searched. Had those agents shown up on Saturday morning instead of Sunday morning they would have been met at the door by an associate of mine that had 15 pounds of marijuana in his car, a half an ounce of cocaine on a tray under his bed and an unlicensed gun. We would have all gone to jail.

Because I had not sold a controlled substance I was placed on probation and did not ever set foot in jail. The day of the raid I was released on my own recognizance. Two months later I met the man who would eventually become my husband. Four years later I was in full-time ministry.

God promised my mother He would be a husband to her and a Father to her children. He promised her there would be angels encamped around us lest we dash our foot against a stone. He promised her He would keep us as the apple of His eye. He didn't promise it would always be easy or we would always make the right choices. He did promise He would always be there waiting lovingly and patiently until we made the only choice that really matters, the choice to accept Jesus Christ as Lord and Saviour! He will never leave you, nor forsake you, no matter how far away you think you've gone. He's waiting right now for you to tell Him you love Him and you need Him in your life.

Be prepared for tomorrow's
encounters by obeying God today.

You Are Not Alone

Know that you are not alone
For I am in your heart
I have sent My angels
To guide you through the dark.

As fear creeps in
You know just what to do
Pick up My Word
Let Me flow through you.

A comfort My Words will be
Let them help you to laugh and sing
Soon My child you will see
What peace and joy My Spirit brings.

Trisha Phelps

CHAPTER SIX

The Beginning of a Miracle

But in a great house there are not only vessels of gold and silver, but also of wood and clay, some for honor and some for dishonor. Therefore if anyone cleanses himself from the latter, he will be a vessel for honor, sanctified and useful for the Master, prepared for every good work.
2 Timothy 2:20-21

My birthday is August 11th and Kent always does something nice for me, but the year of 1993 was so busy we didn't celebrate until October 3rd. He took me on a wonderful cruise on the Grand Romance cruise ship and we had the best night. Dinner was wonderful and in between courses we sat on the back of the ship and enjoyed a spectacular Florida sunset criss-crossing the evening sky with hues of pink, purple and orange. It was indeed a night to remember.

It was a late night for us but we knew we could sleep in the next morning. We had a trip planned to head over to Ormond Beach for the day and we were looking forward to it. But more importantly I had finally started to plan the trip to see my father the following week. I am an early riser so when I awoke at 6:30 a.m. I relaxed knowing I didn't have to get up right away.

My next realization was the reason I had awakened was because my head really hurt. I had been sleeping on my right side and it dawned on me that the whole right side of my face was numb and so was my right shoulder, arm and hand. I figured I had slept on that side wrong and what I needed was a jolt of caffeine to get rid of that headache. As I stood up my balance was off and my left eye seemed to be out of focus. By this time a little niggling fear made its way into the back of my mind but I shrugged it off with a laugh and told myself no more late nights out, I was getting too old for it. I didn't mention any of this to my husband and we went on to the beach as planned. The numbness did subside as the day went on but my eye never did focus and the pain in my head had become a very persistent dull ache.

As we were leaving that afternoon we were in two different cars and I was to drive with Peg, Kent's mom. As I got behind the wheel I knew my eye was in bad shape but I drove on. Our destination was Wal-Mart, mine and Caleb's favorite place to spend time. Our objective was to find Caleb one more toy from Me-maw and Pa-paw! As soon as we walked in my head exploded. I told Kent I needed to sit down and he was just shocked. Usually I would have put him in the wind and been headed for the closest aisle.

By now we were both concerned so he called his sister Ann who is a nurse. He described all of the symptoms I'd had since waking up and she very calmly suggested we go to the nearest hospital and get me checked out. She said she didn't want to be an alarmist but it sounded as though I may be having a slight brain bleed. Well, there it was right out in the open. What

I had been trying to avoid thinking all day had finally been said out loud. Kent told me to sit and calmly left to tell his parents we were going to the hospital.

Once we arrived and he told the emergency personnel what he had just explained to his sister a lot of activity began to occur. I was already in a wheel chair and I knew that if they came over and slapped one of those little plastic bracelets on my wrist I was going to be admitted. As crazy as it sounds I had an overwhelming desire to tell the nurse as she was putting it on, thank you, but that doesn't match my outfit. I kept that to myself which was probably a good thing. They might have sent me to the psychiatric ward.

The next thing to happen was a change of wardrobe so now my outfit was completely coordinated. The little number was cotton and conveniently designed to open in the back. An aide showed us to our emergency suite and helped me onto an examining table.

I will never forget how cold it was. The whole place was freezing and by now I was trembling with fear. It took quite awhile for the ER doctor to show up so I made a powder room run. Kent wheeled me down and as I walked in, I got a glimpse of my new outfit. I looked in the mirror and asked God, "What in the world is going on now?" I was talking right out loud and I said, "Just look at me, 24 hours ago I was on a cruise ship having a ball in my favorite black dress and here I am in a backless hospital gown. What is the deal?"

It was one of those times He was stone cold silent. Even though He wasn't saying anything, His silence spoke volumes. I knew enough about God's way of doing things to realize He was trying to get my attention. Trust me, by this time I was standing up and paying attention.

As Kent wheeled me back to our uninviting little cubicle I noticed my husband was doing all he could do to be brave. I knew right then we both had to get a grip, so we did. We prayed and even though God was still being quiet we felt more at peace. It's a good thing we prayed when we did.

Right after we released this whole situation to the Lord the ER doctor came in. He was very young and proceeded to tell us how qualified he was to be treating me. He was very hyper and paced up and down while he explained all of the different things that could be wrong with me. He ended his summation with a brief explanation of a brain bleed. In effect he said, "Once they found it, I could be fine for awhile and then drop dead while on holiday somewhere." Qualified he may have been, but his bedside manner left something to be desired.

I thought Kent was going to croak. At this point I was more worried about him than I was about me. We had prayed but he shifted into battle position, calling every person we knew, drawing the battle lines. We began to pray and agree and the power of God began to flow. The Lord gave him the scripture that turned us around during this time of prayer.

Psalm 128:1-6 kept us strong. This scripture tells us of the blessings of those who fear the Lord. "Blessed is every one of us who fears the Lord. Who walks in His ways. When you eat the labor of your own hands, you shall be happy, and it shall be well with you. Your wife shall be like a fruitful vine. In the very heart of your house, your children like olive plants all around your table, behold, thus shall the man be blessed who fears the Lord. The Lord bless you out of Zion, and may you see the good of Jerusalem all the days of your life. Yes, may you see your children's children." Kent clung to the fruitful vine and I held onto the future grandchildren.

Around 3 a.m. my room in critical care was ready and I received yet another accessory to complete my ensemble. A heart monitor was taped to my chest. As I took in my new surroundings it really hit home how sick they must have thought I was.

All around me was very serious medical equipment and in the next bed was an elderly lady who just cried and cried. Every three or four minutes she would ring her little buzzer and ask the nurse if it was time for her to go home yet. They weren't giving any definite answers and to tell the truth I was starting to feel like my neighbor. When was I going to get to go home? She kept crying and the nurses made Josh and Kent leave. They gave me a light sedative and I passed out.

The next morning the neurologist came in and explained what they had found on the initial X-ray. It seemed to show something they needed to check out a bit further so he was scheduling a cat scan, a spinal tap and possibly an MRI, depending on what the spinal tap turned up. Have you ever been so cold that perspiration drops seem hot? That is the only way I can explain the fear that was racing through every pore of my body. I felt fairly rational but fear was trying to take over.

The nurse that wheeled me down asked my husband to please wait in the corridor and she expertly handed me my file and off we went. I say expertly because she acted as though it was common procedure to hand the patient (me) her own file. She pushed me down to the correct room and promptly left me there with the file still in my hot little hands. What would you have done?

Well, I read it, or at least part of it. By the time I had deciphered the medical jargon and made out the part about there being an unidentified shadow on the left side of my brain, she was back, and boy was she ever upset! It seems that files are off limits to patients and she could be fired if my doctor found out I had read any of it. When I asked her why she had left it with me I was sure she muttered something under her breath I didn't need to hear so I didn't ask again. Besides, I had other things on my mind like this unidentified shadow and the nine-inch needle they planned to identify it with!

The procedure itself went well enough. I had a really large talk with the Lord during the spinal tap and I asked Him if He didn't mind would He please fill me in on what was happening. He was still very quiet. I was okay after it was over and I managed to stay still and upright for the next eight hours, just like the doctor had asked of me. Remember, too, I was fairly heavily sedated.

The next morning when the doctor was on the floor I decided I should freshen up before I saw him. My friends that know me well know that I am never seen without mascara. Have you ever seen the commercial that says seven out of ten doctors say they would take Tylenol to a deserted island? Not me, it would be waterproof mascara. Well, I did my make-up and in came the doctor. I don't know for sure what he was expecting but it seemed to be a good sign I looked so well and so rested. As a matter of fact, he was so impressed with my physical appearance and the result of the spinal tap he moved me from critical care to a regular room. I was thrilled, still sedated, but thrilled.

The next test to be done was the CAT scan. I figured I had passed the spinal tap with flying colors, not to mention surviving the nine-inch needle. I was now elated. The sedative was wearing off but not quite enough for me to realize how traumatized my body was.

Yet another nurse prepared me for the CAT scan. I had no idea what to expect and no one had a pleasant, informative chat with me like they did to prepare me for the needle. Remember, I hadn't moved on my own for about ten hours by this time.

My husband helped me into the wheel chair and we waited. I told him I felt a bit queasy and he rang for the nurse. The desk nurse said it would be a few minutes so we waited. As feeling returned to my body, nausea hit full force. I could not hold my head up. By the time the nurse got there I was really sick. She said it would be best to have the test done because my doctor really needed the results to find out what was wrong with me. That seemed reasonable so we forged ahead.

Hospitals are filled with all kinds of smells and each one I came into contact with assailed my senses with what seemed to be a personal vendetta. By the time we reached our destination I was so weak I simply could not hold myself up. Kent asked for a pain medication for me and the nurse left, presumably to get it.

The young girl who was to do the CAT scan lifted me out of the wheelchair as gently as she could. I was crying out loud by now and Kent was pacing the floor. About twenty minutes had passed and the nurse was nowhere in sight with the medication. The poor girl doing the test was trying to explain what she was doing as she parted my hair and stuck little pieces of what looked like Play-Dough on my scalp.

To the Play-Dough she attached electrodes and then she hooked me up to the machine. God knows how hard I tried to sit up so she could do the test but I was crying so hard and my body felt as though I had been on a boat in high seas for about a month. Kent came over to hold me up and I will never forget staring down at his shoes and asking him to please tell me what was happening to me.

Three days ago I had been a perfectly healthy woman and now I couldn't hold myself up. Then I threw up on his shoes. I don't know what shook him up more, the fact I couldn't hold myself up or I had thrown up on him. I hope you are really getting a good visual of the scene being played out here.

Bear in mind I still had all of those electrodes sticking straight out of my head. The nurse still hasn't shown up despite numerous calls from the technician and now I have ruined Kent's shoes. There was nothing left to do but pray.

We prayed for strength to get us through this situation and then the nurse finally put in an appearance and mercifully gave me a shot that knocked me out.

Once I was back in my room the doctor was called and it turned out that I was having an incredibly bad reaction to the spinal tap. My doctor thought because I looked so well that I had made it through the tough part without any problems. For the remainder of my stay, I went au naturale. I looked as bad as I felt. As I've mentioned to you, God wanted my attention and I was beginning to understand it was my undivided attention He desired.

The final test needed was the MRI. Have I told you yet how incredibly claustrophobic I am? The MRI test is done in a machine that is shaped remarkably like a coffin. Had I known this bit of information I don't think I would have made the decision to have one performed. The day after the CAT scan episode I was just as sick.

The aftereffects of a spinal tap can last up to seven days. I was on day three. Medication had been prescribed to help with the pain and I was mostly out of it. Once again I was loaded up for a ride but this time I was on a gurney. The wheelchair was just too difficult for me to manage. The nurses loaded me up and wheeled me out into the middle of the ward by the elevators. They told Kent someone from across the street would pick me up.

As I lay there drifting in and out of reality, bits of conversation filtered through. Kent kept asking how long it was going to be and the nurse on the floor kept saying she didn't know. I had pulled the sheet over my eyes because it was so bright in the hall. I could feel people walking right by my head and I started to feel really anxious.

Kent's tone of voice was getting rather strident and I knew he was getting more upset by the minute. Finally, he went over and demanded the nurse call to find out what was taking so long. She didn't want to do it but finally she called.

It turned out there was no one scheduled to pick up a patient for MRI testing that day so they recruited a couple of orderlies from that floor. We didn't realize the test was to be done in an entirely different building and we had no idea it was a block away.

The conversation between the orderlies went something like this, 1st orderly: "Hey man, do you know where we're going?" Second orderly: "Naw man, I'm from New York, I just been here a couple of weeks." About that time they wheeled me over the curb. Kent asked them if they were kidding about not knowing where the building was. They said no and my husband suggested they find out in a hurry. So, they started reading the signs out loud to him. We all found the building together.

When it was all over Kent told me that the reason he was so nervous was because the whole time I had been waiting for someone to pick me up there had been construction workers walking by my head with hammers hanging out of their aprons!

For some reason that opened my eyes to what was really going on. God was trying to get my attention and He was allowing me to be tested! I had made the decision to go see my dad but my heart wasn't right. Therefore, I was left vulnerable to an attack of the enemy.

In Job 1:8 God asks Satan, "Have you considered my servant Job, that there is none like him on earth, a blameless and upright man, one who fears God and shuns evil?" Verse nine continues, "So Satan answered the Lord and said, 'Does Job fear God for nothing? Have you not made a hedge around him, around his household, and around all that he has on every side? You have blessed the work of his hands, and his possessions have increased in the land.'"

In verse 12 the Lord obviously makes the decision to allow Satan to test His faithful servant Job because He says, "Satan, behold all that he has is in your power, only do not lay a hand on his person." Here we see God putting very definite limits on Satan's power. Satan cannot touch us without God's divine permission. I was neither blameless nor righteous and I believe God was refining me.

My brother-in-law, Danny, a pastor for 23 years, does a wonderful teaching on the refining process of gold. Before there were modern methods of heating gold to the point silt could be culled off, men just kept adding more and more heat to the pot and when the dross rose to the top it was ladled off. The process continued until their faces could be seen in the gold.

That is a perfect analogy of going through the fire. God just keeps adding more heat until He sees His face reflecting back at Him. Satan is actually powerless until God gives him permission to throw a little more fire our way.

In my Spirit-Filled Life Bible these points are addressed and I think they will be a help to you in understanding God's times of trials and testing.

1. Choose to trust God's absolute sovereignty in any adversity.

2. Understand that while God may allow us to be tested, He sets strict limits on the tests.

3. Believe that the Lord examines all your ways.

4. Know that God's works are often unfathomable by the human mind.

5. Understand that Christ is our advocate with the Father.

6. Know our case is hopeless without Him.

7. Understand God is the creator of all men.

8. Understand that God is totally righteous in what He renders to man and totally free from wrongdoing.

9. Know and understand God as creator and sustainer of the universe.

10. Know and learn that He, not you, determines what is right.

11. Avoid resentment and unforgiveness and envy. Believe that they are destructive attitudes.

12. Embrace the Lord's correction. Consider it a blessing and know that it evidences the Lord's love for you.

Truth-In-Action Section, Spirit-Filled Life Bible (Job)

Of course, I've come to these realizations over time, but that day in the hospital all I knew was God had not been getting the reflection He wanted and the fire was getting hotter and hotter. I repented right there and asked God to forgive me for my attitude and I shook my fist at Satan and told him that if I had to make the trip to Maury, North Carolina in an ambulance I was going to see my father and I was going to ask him to forgive me and I was going to forgive him!

That decision was really the beginning of true healing for me. We still had a few more fires to put out and looking back over the past three years it is really almost comical viewing them with the advantage of passing time.

The trip to see my father had been planned for quite a while and we had been saving money. That was the first thing to go. We had been living off of the saved money the week I spent in the hospital. The next expense was the air conditioner in the car. Then slowly, one by one, our appliances all went. The washing machine was first, then our ice-maker in the freezer and finally my oven just quit working. With each new financial burden I became more determined.

When the time came to leave for Maury Correctional Center we were facing a twelve-hour drive and I still could not hold my head up. The only repair that had been made was on the air-conditioner in our car and we had an additional passenger we had not planned on.

Because of my unexpected stay in the hospital I didn't have the heart to leave Caleb for another week. It had been a scary experience for all of us and Caleb didn't understand why I had been in the hospital at all. I, on the other hand, understood it perfectly.

When the motivation of my heart changed the healing process began physically. The shadow was gone and my diagnosis was a complicated optical, tension migraine. My doctor said it was stress related and I believed him, but the stress was nothing compared to the relief I felt when he told me what they had found.

I believe with all of my heart that God healed me and what could have developed into a life-threatening tumor was removed because I made the choice to forgive. You see, God has a plan for each of our lives and to fulfill the call God has on each of us we really must be as empty vessels, waiting to be filled with the Spirit of God.

When we are carrying all of the bondage's and burdens of the past there is little or no room for God to work through us. I'd like to invite you now to look deeply into your own life and check to make sure you aren't carrying a load that is too heavy. See if perhaps your vessel has developed a few cracks and what you have managed to hold onto has developed a slow leak.

Maybe what has been going into your vessel has become bitter and it is poisoning other areas of your life. If this is happening to you, take time to evaluate where the pain is coming from and ask the Holy Spirit to reveal the root of it.

Asking for forgiveness and releasing someone from unforgiveness is a daily choice. It may not seem as though anything has changed. The important thing is you have confessed it to God and He is working on your behalf.

A few weeks ago a woman asked me exactly how does a person walk in forgiveness. As I looked at her, I saw how much she desired to be walking closer to the Lord. The first thing I encouraged her to do was to release the situation to Him. Next I shared with her that we must choose to forgive and release those who have hurt us by forgiving them. She was listening to every word intensely. Next, and most importantly, you must pray for them and bless those who have hurt us and believe God is healing our emotions. As I talked to her she got really excited and asked how she would know if it was working. This is the part that was hard for me too.

I wanted to see fruit right away, but sometimes we must wait for the fruit and know that the Master Gardener is still pruning some of our branches. In John 15, verses 4-5, 7-9 and 11, the Word of God makes this very clear. "Abide in Me, and I in you. As the branch cannot bear fruit of itself, except it abide in the vine; no more can ye, except ye abide in Me. I am the vine, you are the branches; He that abideth in Me, and I in him, the same bringeth forth much fruit; for without Me ye can do nothing... If ye abide in Me, and My words abide in you, ye shall ask what you will, and it shall be done unto you. Herein is My Father glorified that ye bear much fruit; so shall ye be My disciples. As the Father hath loved Me, so I have loved you, continue in My love... These things have I spoken unto you, that My joy might remain in you, and that your joy might be full."

The only way we will see the fruit of forgiveness is to trust completely that God's Word is true and trust Him to do the work. The bitter root of unforgiveness must be released to God joyfully. That's where I got into trouble.

In Charles Stanley's teaching on the Power of Love, Dr. Stanley states, "God is not afraid to love us... He is secure enough to love us unconditionally. There is no conditional love with God. Stop counting the injustices done against you. Once you do this, love is set in motion and the Holy Spirit begins His work." I released my hurts and wounds to my heavenly Father, but conditionally. My behavior was unacceptable to God. He did not want me to see my father with a hard heart. He wanted me to be soft and pliable, like potter's clay. He was reshaping my vessel into one He could use.

We continued on with our plans for the trip and even though I really was still very weak physically, I felt stronger in my spirit than I ever had before. The trip there was a long one and I made most of it lying down in the back seat of the car. With each passing mile, fear and apprehension tried to attack my mind. I concentrated on Caleb and asked the Holy Spirit to please give me the words to speak once we had arrived. Truly, I will never forget that day as long as I live.

*Be confident God has a plan when trials
and suffering are causing discouragement.*

An Evening Prayer

If I have wounded any soul today,
If I have caused one foot to go astray,
If I have walked in my own willful way
Good Lord, forgive.
If I have uttered idle words or vain,
If I have turned aside from want or pain
Lest I myself should suffer through the strain
Good Lord, forgive.
If I have craved for joys that are not mine,
If I have let my wayward heart repine
Dwelling on things on earth, not things divine
Good Lord, forgive.
Forgive the sins I have confessed to Thee,
Forgive the secret sins I do not see;
That which I know not, Father, teach Thou me
Help me to live.

C. Maude Bathersby

CHAPTER SEVEN

Why Don't I Feel Free?

For we are His workmanship, created in Christ
Jesus for good works, which God prepared
beforehand that we should walk in them.
Ephesians 2:10

I started work on this manuscript three and a half years ago. The Lord put it in my heart to do it but I didn't have the faith for it. As I put the words on paper I kept saying if only I had done this or if this would happen, then I could really get some work done.

There were many things in my life that I based the result on some ambiguous circumstance that would bring every thing in my life into one accord. For example, there was our house. We have been remodeling this house since the day we moved in on April 1, 1988. There was so much to do all I could see was the huge amount of work.

No matter how much progress was made there was always

something else to rip out, paint, tile or put border on. I couldn't enjoy any of the results of our labors because I was so focused on the finished product.

I have come to realize that when you own a home, to some degree it will always be a work in progress. That's how it is in our Christian walk as well. We are works in progress. "We are to press toward the mark of the high calling of God in Christ Jesus" Philippians 3:14.

That is so true. We are to press on, but before we can press on we must press in. There is not a fast-food equivalent to God's kingdom. To know Him and to know His heart we must spend time with Him.

Before I was reconciled to my father, I'd say, "Lord, change him so I can handle seeing him." I said a lot of things to the Lord during that period of my life. I hope He edited them off my record.

Never, not once, did I say, "Lord, change me so he can handle seeing me." Even after I saw my father I wasn't able to go back to writing this book because I wanted, as Paul Harvey says, the rest of the story.

Like so many others that I have known over the years I had lived the better part of my adult life trying to live down my past, and was still battling just to make it through my present and was putting all my hope in the future.

The problem was I still was not walking in the blessing the Lord wanted me to have right here on earth. "Eye hath not seen, nor ear heard, neither have entered into the heart of man, the things which God hath prepared for them that love Him" 1 Corinthians 2:9. I felt like I had to get to the next level of spirituality to really please God. I wanted my father to be saved before I wrote this book. But God's ways are not man's ways.

I talked about this issue constantly. (Remember, every one has an issue.) It was depressing, it was too hard to be so transparent and tell all those sordid details about my past. The more I talked about it the less inclined I was to do anything about it. So, for two years it stayed in a folder in the back of my desk.

During this two-year period a lot of healing took place between my father, myself and the whole rest of my family. It was as if the floodgates of the healing power of forgiveness was being poured straight from heaven onto my entire family. Then I decided I couldn't write it because my father would think badly of me for telling all the family secrets. The enemy did not want this story told. I kept telling anyone that would listen that I'd finish it when my father was saved.

Finally, Kent got the revelation! He said, "Bev, the miracle is not your father's SALVATION, the miracle is your FORGIVENESS!!!" Well, a small light did begin to burn when he said that but it wasn't until this past January that the small light turned into a fire.

Pastor Benny Hinn's monthly crusades are held all over the United States and I try to go to at least one a year. The crusade for January was being held in Honolulu, Hawaii. Kent had been to Hawaii several times but I had never been so I was really excited about going. This was a particularly special trip because I had a friend in Honolulu that I had not seen since I was a teenager. We had plans to have lunch but I was really hoping she would join us for the evening service.

From Honolulu we went on to Maui and even though I didn't see much of my husband I still had a wonderful time. The highlight of the trip was meeting Dr. Oral Roberts and his lovely wife, Evelyn. The rest of the team was going home a day earlier than we were so we had been given the wonderful opportunity of spending time with them.

The first day after the Roberts' arrival Miss Evelyn, as she is affectionately known by the people that know and love her, invited Patsy Brock, Connie Haus and myself to go to lunch. The four of us hired a taxi and headed into town.

I would be less than truthful if I didn't tell you I was thrilled! Miss Evelyn is such a gracious lady and to have the opportunity to spend time with her was a very exciting prospect. My dear friend Patsy got so tickled with me because I kept whispering, "That's EVELYN ROBERTS up there in the front seat!" Patsy has been saved her whole life and was raised as a pastor's daughter but she did tell me later that it was also very exciting for her as well.

We had a beautiful lunch and a great time of fellowship. Miss Evelyn shared some wonderful stories with us. It is still hard for me to comprehend how God took me with all of my shortcomings and history and placed me in the ministry.

One of my favorite passages of scripture in the entire Bible is Paul the Apostle sharing his heart with Timothy. "And I thank Christ Jesus, our Lord, who hath enabled me, for that He counted me faithful, putting me into the ministry; who was before a blasphemer, and a persecutor, and injurious, but I obtained mercy because I did it ignorantly in unbelief. And the grace of our Lord was exceeding abundant with faith and love which is in Christ Jesus. This is a faithful saying and worthy of all acceptation that Christ Jesus came into the world to save sinners; of whom I am chief" 1 Timothy 1:12-15.

It is sometimes so overwhelming to consider where I started out and where I am now. I thank God every day of my life that I am not going to hell. Salvation is still the greatest miracle of all. That day, as I looked around the table, I saw the joy of the Lord on each one of those precious ladies' faces. They were all in full-time ministry and had been for all their lives. Our talk was full of where we've been and what God has done for us. Needless to say, I could have won the vote for the most diversified!

Later that day after Dr. Roberts returned from taping shows for Pastor Benny's daily broadcast, "This Is Your Day," Kent and I had the privilege of talking with the Roberts for awhile. Dr. Roberts said he would like to pray for us before we left and of course, we were agreeable

He prayed for me first and prayed a strong prayer for me to conceive because Kent and I have been trying to have another baby for several years. He then prayed for my husband and we were both very blessed and honored.

We both thought he was through but he turned to me again and said, "I see you at your work. Your head is bent over and you are in the typing position." He then demonstrated how I looked. He continued to pray and said, "When you are at your work a spirit of depression attacks your mind and you can't finish it."

As he prayed I saw myself at the computer terminal in the accounting office at church and I was sitting in the same position he had just shown me, so I thought that was what he was seeing. As he prayed, he began to rebuke the spirit of depression and cast it out. He turned to me and said, "You will never battle that spirit of depression again!"

As we left, Kent and I pondered what had just happened. All of a sudden we both got really excited and Kent said, "Bev, it isn't your work in the accounting office." (I had already figured that out because I loved doing that particular job.) "God just showed him you at work on your book!" We both knew that was my true work that God had called me to do, and I had been battling depression!

The next morning we told the Roberts about the book and how God had used him to deliver me from depression. Then,

Dr. Roberts got excited and told us God was in this book and I needed to go home and finish it. That was on January 16, 1995. I have been working nonstop since then. It has been the most amazing and exciting experience. I no longer feel my story is a source of shame and embarrassment.

Kent was right about the true miracle having already occurred. It happened the moment my heart melted with love and forgiveness for my father. It happened in that split second that my spiritual shackles came off. It happened when God replaced my "heart of stone with a heart of flesh" Ezekiel 36:26.

Jesus will meet every need if
you will just believe.

Think first of someone else.
Appreciate, be kind, be gentle.
Laugh a little more.
Deserve confidence.
Take up arms against malice.
Decry complacency.
Express your gratitude.
Worship your God.
Gladden the heart of a child.
Take pleasure in the beauty and wonder of the earth.
Speak your love.
Speak it again.
Speak it still again.
Speak it still once again.

Author Unknown

CHAPTER EIGHT

Riches Beyond Measure

*Above all things have intense and unfailing
love for one another, for love covers a
multitude of sins (forgives and disregards
the offenses of others).*
1 Peter 4:8

It's a beautiful May morning and I'm already out on our screened back porch sweeping and praying over my sleeping household. The smell of brewing coffee is drifting out reminding me I haven't had a cup yet.

The familiar sounds of our neighborhood are beginning to make themselves heard. The 6:45 a.m. school bus is idling on the corner, waiting for all the children to board. The recycling truck is on it's way down the street and Josh's alarm is just going off. Without even looking I can tell you Josh has already burrowed back under his big fluffy comforter and all six feet and three inches of him is covered from head to toe.

In Caleb's bed, the covers are most likely on the floor and even in his sleep he is ready for whatever adventure the day may bring. I cherish this early morning time alone with God because my blessings are displayed as though they were beautiful gemstones and God Himself has placed them to show their glorious richness and colors.

For many years the fullness of God's blessings in my life were obscured by the emotions that kept me bound. My perspective was like a photograph that focuses too sharply on one subject and causes everything else to be a blurred version of what the camera's eye was trying to capture.

I had internalized so many emotions for so long that even though I was present and participating in the activities in my loved one's lives physically, my mind and emotions were thousands of miles away from the experiences that should have brought joy and fulfillment to my life.

When you live with a wound so deep that it consumes and shapes every area of your life it is impossible to understand the blessings of God. It took years for me to really understand how devastated I was when my father went to prison.

True, I did feel a sense of freedom from the violence and his rages, but at the same time there was a tremendous sense of abandonment and loss of protection. My father may have been a threat to his own family but I wanted to believe he would stop outside forces from harming any of us.

My own sense of abandonment came from him actually being removed from the home. Even though he was not physically in our home very often, I didn't feel a real sense of loss until he was really gone. I felt so let down that it was very difficult to trust anyone with my emotions.

The unforgiveness that actually severed my relationship with my father and prevented me from knowing God as my heavenly Father was a bitter root that never allowed me to walk in or understand the blessings God had for me. A real part of my healing process was understanding that my natural father had no concept of the blessings of God either. He couldn't teach them to his family because he didn't know that God wanted to bless him.

When I came to the understanding that my father didn't know how to be blessed by God it opened my eyes to how important it really is for me to walk in absolute, unwavering love and forgiveness for my father.

In the book of Matthew, chapter 18, verses 21-35 we see the Lord Jesus Christ patiently explaining to Peter the importance of forgiveness:

"Then came Peter to Him and said Lord, how oft shall my brother sin against me, and I forgive him? til seven times? Jesus saith unto him, 'I say not unto thee, until seven times but until seventy times seven. Therefore is the kingdom of heaven likened unto a certain king, which would take account of his servants. And when he had begun to reckon, one was brought unto him, which owed him ten thousand talents ($52,800,000 if it was silver). But forasmuch as he had not to pay, his lord commanded him to be sold, and his wife, and children, and all that he had, and payment to be made. The servant fell down and worshipped him, saying, Lord, have patience with me, and I will pay thee all. Then the lord of that servant was moved with compassion, and loosed him and forgave him that debt. But the same servant went out and found one of his fellow servants, which owed him an hundred pence ($44) and took him by the throat, saying, pay me that thou owest. And his fellow servant fell at his feet, and besought him, saying, have patience with me, and I will pay thee all, and he would not; but went and cast him into prison, til he should pay his debt. So when his fellow servants saw what was done, they were very sorry,

and came and told unto their lord all that was done. Then his lord after that he had called him, said unto him, O thou wicked servant, I forgave thee all that debt, because thou desirest me; shouldest not thou also had compassion on thy fellow servant, even as I had pity on thee? And his lord was wroth, and delivered him to the tormentors, till he should pay all that was due him. So likewise shall my heavenly father do also unto you, if you from your hearts forgive not every one his brother their trespasses."

In my estimation of my relationship with my father I was exactly like the unforgiving servant. For years I had sympathy for my father but I had no compassion. There is no action with sympathy. I did not do anything to display a Christlike attitude. It was only when I began to see my father through the love of Christ that I was able to have compassion for him and begin to take action and love him.

In gathering information for this book I came across an editorial that was written after my father was sentenced to a life sentence in prison. At the time of sentencing he was thirty-eight years old, one year younger than I am now.

In reading that editorial I realized for the first time what a tortured existence my father had lived. The reporter took all of his information from court files and started from the time my father was eighteen years old until the sentencing when he was thirty-nine. Over a twenty-year period he was arrested no less than forty times. The crimes ranged from public disturbances to breaking and entering. There is a gradual progression of the seriousness of the crimes, starting with very petty teenage trouble, ending in a life sentence for first degree murder.

Throughout his life of being in and out of trouble he also married and had five children that have always been under the weight of the decisions and choices he made. It was a heavy weight to bear and I was all too eager to lay it down. Unfortunately, I couldn't let go of all the pain until God clearly showed me that the only way I could really walk in true forgiveness was to truly forgive. Matthew 6:14-15 says, "For if ye forgive men their trespasses, your heavenly Father will also forgive you; but if ye forgive not men their trespasses, neither will your Father forgive your trespasses."

I had to trust the Holy Spirit to help me love and forgive because I didn't feel loving or forgiving. It is a part of renewing your mind daily in the Word of God. Once I began to confess forgiveness for my father it became easier to walk in forgiveness.

Once I was able to express how angry, abandoned, rejected, bitter and hurt I had been for all of those years, my heavenly Father was able to begin working in me. I started to feel blessed and to know God's hand was on my life, not just because I was reading it in the Bible but because I was living it!

Over the years I have written down many of my thoughts and experiences in a journal. In the eight and a half years I have been saved there have been so many changes and opportunities for growth. As I read my journals I literally watch a new creature in Christ being born. There have been setbacks and missed opportunities for spiritual growth but I see God's handprint shaping and molding me into that much desired image of His precious son.

Like you, I am constantly working toward that prize but in the meantime I have learned to recognize God's blessings and to enjoy them. Several months ago I was having a particularly good time with the Lord in prayer and I decided to write down all God has given me. To make it interesting I used the alphabet and listed everything I could think of and thanked God for His abundant blessings in my life. I enjoyed doing it so much I'm going to share it with you and perhaps you will want to make your own list.

God Has Given to Me:

A. Abundant life; Amazing grace

B. The Blood of Jesus

C. The Comforter; my son Caleb

D. Deliverance from bondage

E. Eternal life

F. Forgiveness; Faithfulness

G. Grace

H. A godly Heritage for our children

I. The Indwelling presence of the Holy Spirit

J. Joy; my son Josh

K. Knowledge; my husband Kent

L. Love

M. Mercy

N. My Needs are met

O. The desire to be Obedient

P. Patience

Q. Quiet times with Him

R. Rest in Him

S. Success from my failures

T. Treasures

U. Understanding

V. Value

W. Worth

X. X-citement!

Y. Yearnings for more of Him

Z. Zeal; Zest for life

Romans 4:7 says, "Blessed are they whose iniquities are forgiven and whose sins are covered." I pray you are able to use every letter in the alphabet and are running over with blessings. If there are still areas in your life you are working through, remember to pray for those who have hurt you, confess you have forgiven them and let the Holy Spirit do the rest.

Healthy self-love generates a healthy love of others. Love yourself.

Daily Creed

Let me be a little kinder,
Let me be a little blinder to the faults of those about me.
Let me praise a little more.
Let me be, when I am weary, just a little bit more cheery;
Let me serve a little better, the God we would adore.
Let me be a little meeker with the brother who is weaker;
Let me strive a little harder to be all that I should be.
Let me be more understanding, and a little less demanding.
Let me be the sort of friend that you have always been to me.

John Gray

CHAPTER NINE

Hope for Tomorrow

For I am not ashamed of the gospel of Christ,
for it is the power of God to salvation for
everyone who believes...
Romans 1:16

In the book, *When God Whispers Your Name*, author Max Lucado writes, "I've often thought it strange that Matthew would begin his book with a genealogy...But then again, Matthew wasn't a journalist and the Holy Spirit wasn't trying to get our attention. He was making a point. God had promised He would give a Messiah through the bloodline of Abraham (Genesis 12:3), and He did. "Having doubts about the future?" Matthew asks. "Just take a look at the past." And with that he opens the cedar chest of Jesus' lineage and begins to pull out dirty linen.

Isaiah 43:18-19 says, "Remember ye not the former things neither consider the things of old. Behold, I will do a new thing;

now it shall spring forth, shall ye not know it? I will even make a way in the wilderness and rivers in the desert." I believe God gave us this scripture to reveal that no matter what has occurred in the times past that He is ready and willing to bring you into a time of refreshing and pour Himself out onto you. God wants to rebuild your life just as He did the nation of Judah (1 Samuel 8:5,20) when He began to build the lives of the people after their captivity and return.

In reading Jesus' genealogy God began to show me that He personally sent our Lord Jesus through a bloodline that was filled with liars, cheaters, murderers, prostitutes and generally unsavory people. Why do you think He chose such a group of people for the living God to descend from? Hosea 4:1-2 tells us, "There is no faithfulness or kindness and no knowledge of God in the land; there is swearing, lying, killing, stealing and committing adultery; they break all bounds and murder follows murder." This is a prophetic word for the house of Israel, but it is also the time we are living in.

For my entire life I had dealt with the shame of having a father that lived his life outside of not only man's laws but God's laws as well. The problem was that I ended up living on the wrong side of the law just as he had done and I was repeating the pattern that had been established by his actions. In her book, *Door of Hope*, Jan Frank uses the example of Eli and Samuel's relationship to demonstrate how we carry patterns from one generation to the next.

In Exodus 34:6-7 and 1 Samuel 1-3, Eli failed to restrain his sons and as a result God pronounced judgment on Eli's house. Samuel was used, even as a child, to deliver the message of judgment to Eli.

Although Samuel was a prophet ordained by God, he too, failed to learn the negative lesson exemplified in Eli's life. In 1 Samuel 8:1-3 we read that Samuel appointed his sons as judges over Israel but his sons walked not in his ways, but turned aside after lucre (money) and took bribes and perverted judgment.

Exodus 34:6-7 says, "the sins of the fathers are visited upon their children and upon their children's children unto the third and fourth generations." I have seen this principle work in my own family and in my life. Even though I was ashamed of my father's actions and behavior patterns I continued to repeat them until I was born again. Frankly, it was a real struggle for me to be free even after I was saved. The obvious signs of being in the world started to disappear but I still had so much anger and a fierce spirit of pride.

As a child one of my greatest sources of fear was the look of anger my father could convey to get my attention. Just one glimpse of those glaring blue eyes and his jaw tightly clenched would send absolute terror through my whole body. It was enough for him to just look my way and scare me to the point of nausea. But, I can tell you something else that really sickened me.

Not too long ago Caleb was hollering at our dog for chewing something up and I could hear him getting meaner and meaner sounding. By the time they both entered the room I was in and I got a look at his face I was just shocked. There was the same glaring look and set jaw I would have recognized anywhere. It was the same look I had grown up in such terror of.

There is only place he could have seen that look. He was imitating me! I asked God to please forgive me then I asked my precious son to forgive me. I made him promise that if I ever looked at him like that again that he would not be afraid to tell me I had that ugly, scary face. He promised he would and then told me how scary it was for him when I looked like that. I was brokenhearted that I had been scaring him, but most of all I was brokenhearted that I had not realized I was even doing it!

Overcoming anger and acting out in anger has been one of the most difficult parts of the healing process for me. In my family we refer to the anger that overtakes our minds as the "red hole." It is a place born out of despair and helplessness. As an adult I have struggled to never go into that place where anger consumes every rational thought and affects every part of my life. In the book, *Healing Memories*, David Seamands writes, "The harder we try to keep bad memories out of conscious recall, the more powerful they become. Since they are not allowed to enter through the door of our minds directly, they come into our personalities (body, mind and spirit) in disguised and destructive ways."

I was so angry with my father for so long that it became a part of my very being. I was also very fearful of him so I had this vicious cycle of anger, fear, pride and shame affecting me long after I had become a Christian. I have never had any kind of counseling but I have read extensively about how to overcome a hurtful heritage.

One of the best tools I found was the book, *Door of Hope*, by Jan Frank. The Lord gave me the scripture the book is based on many years ago as I was entering into the beginning stages of deliverance and healing. Hosea 2:15 says, "I will...make the Valley of Achor a door of hope." The word Achor means trouble. This verse lets us know that God redeems situations, bringing present hope in the place of previous trouble.

She outlines in this book so many things to draw from in the healing process, but what ministered to me most was the Four Fold Process of Forgiveness. The author states that forgiveness is a process and the more serious the injury the longer it may take to heal. This process helped me and I pray it helps you.

1. Acknowledge the pain. Identify the feelings as your own and assess how they have impacted your life through the suffering they caused.

2. Release your right to hold onto bitterness, resentment and anger. Ask the Lord to help you release any anger, bitterness or resentment that lingers in the depth of your heart.

3. Desire reconciliation. Apply the blood of Jesus that was shed on your behalf to the offense.

4. Extend an invitation to rebuild the damaged relationship through unconditional love and acceptance. Choose an act of kindness that can be extended in sincerity to those who hurt you.

Even though I made the decision to not give in to anger, I was doing it in my own strength. Because of my pride-based shame I wouldn't allow anyone in to help me. Not even my heavenly Father. Growing up I didn't want others to know what went on at home so I hid my emotions and when my father went to prison I stayed far away from anyone that could have helped me.

Like so many people that have a fear of being rejected, I sought out a peer group that would not judge me for my lack of pedigree. The background of the drug culture in the late sixties and early seventies was the perfect escape. We go where we are accepted because as human beings we desire a sense of belonging.

In the book, *His Image...My Image*, Josh McDowell explains that three basic emotional needs are common to all persons. These needs are:

1. The need to feel loved, accepted; to have a sense of belonging.

2. The need to feel acceptable; to have a sense of worthiness.

3. The need to feel adequate; to have a sense of competence.

When you have none of these needs being met they become magnified, larger than life and you begin to despise your own needs. They become a weakness that you don't want revealed to others so your emotions become distorted and out of balance. Patterns you have lived with all of your life by example now begin to manifest in your own life and without even being aware of the decision being made you begin to lose hope that your situation will ever change.

When God began to heal me from the wounds of my past I knew that there would come a time that I would share my testimony in its entirety. I felt so much shame that the actual healing process got off track. What I finally had to get to was the root of pride that was holding me back from complete healing and deliverance.

I was in a meeting and the speaker made the statement that pride is the root of division. I had never heard that before but it made so much sense. God despises pride and it seems that so many of our problems are rooted in the very thing that God hates most! I asked God to please deliver me from the spirit of pride and reveal to me the areas of my life that were being affected by pride.

As my heavenly Father began to show me layer after layer of hurt that I had covered over and over again, I started to understand that every time I came close to allowing anyone to know me I would retreat to my comfort zone and the pretense that none of the events of my life had affected me. I stayed hidden beneath my pride and my abilities.

The more out of control my inner-self felt, the more in control of my surroundings I became. The whole cycle was taking such a toll on my physical body. By the time I actually saw my father my immune system was simply worn down. I knew I had to make the choice to let the Lord continue His work in me if I was ever going to be able to minister effectively. As He revealed the areas I needed to be free from I asked to be healed and set free.

From October through December the year I saw my father for the first time in 16 years, much healing took place and in December I was asked to minister at a women's meeting. The host pastors knew about my father, but I had never shared publicly about being molested.

As the time grew nearer to speak I had an ongoing conversation with the Lord about telling it or not telling it. I prayed and asked the Lord to please give me the courage and the words to share what He wanted shared. I desire to be used of the Lord in any capacity. I read somewhere He can work with anyone except the proud, so I wanted to come to Him humbly and offer myself for His service. I was more than a little nervous.

I started to feel confident the Lord would use me for His glory so I relaxed and planned my message. Up until the day before the meeting I was healthy, confident and sure I had made the right decision. However, the night before I was to speak I became very ill with a sinus infection and on top of that I had an allergic reaction to the antibiotic prescribed to help me. I didn't sleep at all and the enemy came against me with every tactic to keep me from sharing.

After a miserable night I got up to a rainy, gray day. My body was weak and my mind was overwrought. I told the Lord He would have to do the meeting because I was too sick and then I told the enemy he was defeated. I was going!

If it wasn't for the video I wouldn't be able to tell you what

I said that day. By the time I got home my temperature was 101.2. I can tell you the Holy Spirit moved, and when the altar call was given almost every woman in the place came and told of years of hidden abuse that had affected their lives.

The Lord was faithful to me and He worked the whole incident for His glory. He also showed me that the weaker I am, the stronger He is. As long as I come in the name of the Lord He will never leave me nor forsake me.

I know as a speaker that day I was not especially effective, but two years later I am still being stopped by people and told how much the Lord ministered to them when I shared. Proverbs 11:2 tells us, "When pride cometh, then shame; but with the lowly is wisdom." From this verse we learn that with humility comes wisdom.

Pride has the eternal hostility of God but humbling yourself is the key to God's grace. When I was able to break the shackles of pride in my life I started to walk without shame. As I humbled myself before the Lord I was able to experience His grace.

Humility, wisdom and grace, this cycle is how I desire to live my life because it is life. I am no longer ashamed of my hurtful heritage. I am proud to tell anyone who will listen where I have come from and where I am going.

For years I strove to have a perfect life, to be the perfect wife, the perfect mother, the perfect worker, the perfect Christian. I now realize I am in the process of accepting myself as God accepts me. In one of my Daily Guidepost's devotionals Carol Kykendall suggests seeing ourselves in this light:

1. Be complete by being who God uniquely created.

2. Be mature at your own level, where you are in Christ.

3. Be holy by being surrendered in spirit, knowing you are in the process of growing but you will not reach perfection until you are in heaven.

*This is realistic perfection, not
flawless, but forgiven.*

It is an amazing, powerful place where there is faith.
But if the wicked will
Turn from all his sins
That he hath committed,
And keep all my statutes,
And do that which is lawful
And right, he shall surely live,
He shall not die.
All his transgressions that he
Hath committed, they shall not
Be mentioned unto him:
In his righteousness that he hath done
He shall live.

Ezekiel 18:21-22

CHAPTER TEN

Changing Ungodly Heritages

*Ye shall diligently keep the commandments of the
Lord your God, and His testimonies, and His
statutes which He hath commanded thee.
Deuteronomy 6:17*

"Courtesy and personal hygiene classes to be added to the new high school curriculum," read the newspaper article. I couldn't believe what I was reading as the article went on to state so many teen-agers didn't have any training in basic courtesy and hygiene that the only way school officials could see to change this problem was to offer it as a class in school.

The basic fundamentals of kindness, respect, politeness and bathing are not being taught at home so that responsibility is falling on teachers. As parents we are responsible for teaching these very basic concepts to our children but we have a far greater responsibility.

Deuteronomy 6:5-7 states, "And thou shalt love the Lord

thy God with all thine heart and with all thy soul, and with all thy might. And these words, which I command thee this day shall be in thine heart; And thou shalt teach them diligently unto thy children, and shalt talk of them when thou sittest in thine house, and when thou walkest by the way, and when thou liest down, and when thou risest up." In other words we should constantly reinforce that our relationship with the Lord is the most important relationship in our lives.

Deuteronomy 11:26-28 tells us, "Behold, I set before you this day a blessing and a curse; A blessing if ye obey the commandments of the Lord your God, which I command you this day: And a curse, if ye will not obey the commandments of the Lord your God, but turn aside out of the way which I command you this day, to go after other gods, which ye have not known."

The Lord has given us very specific guidelines to live our lives by. We have a choice of being blessed or being cursed. When Moses came down from Mount Sinai with the Ten Commandments the first thing he had to do was destroy the graven image the people had made in his absence.

The fifth commandment in Exodus 20:5 is very clear about God's intentions: "Thou shalt not bow down thyself to them (other god's), nor serve them; for I the Lord thy God am a jealous God, visiting the iniquity of the fathers upon the children unto the third and fourth generations of them that hate Me; and showing mercy unto thousands of them that love Me and keep My commandments."

God wants us to be blessed. He has set principles and precepts for us to live by so that we will be blessed. He has also given us the free will to make the choice to love Him, serve Him and in return receive all that His word promises us.

As the Holy Spirit really began to move in my life and I started to study the Word of God, I realized even though I had always considered myself to be a Christian and had accepted Jesus Christ as my Lord and Savior, I literally knew nothing about the promises of God.

I went to church almost every Sunday from the time I was a little girl until I was about fourteen. All of the Bible stories and parables were taught but I had no concept of making the choice to serve God for any other reason than not going to hell!

My own mother was very faithful to tell us Jesus loved us and to make sure we were in church but there was a vast chasm between understanding the love of Christ and relating His love for me, to why I wasn't going to spend eternity doing a slow burn.

Ephesians 6:12 says, "For we battle not against flesh and blood, but against principalities, against powers, against the rulers of the darkness of this world, against spiritual wickedness in high places." This portion of scripture is warning the body of Christ to not be caught up in the earthly struggles that are common to all of us, but to prayerfully stand against the invisible assignments of the devil that will keep the church distracted from its job of keeping evil driven back so God's will can be accomplished.

In today's society more families are broken apart than ever before. The responsibility of the fathers as head of the household and protector of the family has become a weight too heavy for many men to bear. They simply walk away to create new families and new lives. It's not just the men. Women are leaving behind their former lives as well. The children that are left behind become the responsibilities of other family members, wards of the state or street kids.

In Proverbs 30:11-14 the Word tells us of this generation, "There is a generation that curseth their father and doth not bless their mother. There is a generation that is pure in their own eyes, and yet is not washed from their own filthiness. There is a generation, O how lofty are their eyes! Their eyelids are lifted up. There is a generation, whose teeth are as swords, and their jaw teeth as knives, to devour the poor from off the earth, and the needy from among men." Here is a generation that has turned its back on the teachings of its fathers and mothers and is seeking only to fulfill its own needs regardless of the cost.

By ignoring the Word of God and continuing on the path of fleshly fulfillment the door for spiritual attacks and curses on the next generation is left wide open. Many families have never even been taught the Word because someone in their family tree made the choice generations ago to turn their back on God. Exodus 20:5 states, "For I the Lord thy God am a jealous God, visiting the iniquity of the fathers upon the children unto the third and fourth generations of them that hate me."

In sharing my experience of salvation and healing it became clear to me that I never made any real decisions about what direction my life would take as I was maturing. There was never any thought given to what my future would hold. Each situation that arose was reacted to. I didn't think, I just reacted to whatever scenario was being played out around me.

Both my parents had been raised in church but they weren't trained to teach their children to make godly decisions. I don't remember my father ever going to church with us. He didn't understand his position as the priest of our household and as our spiritual covering.

To know God's Word you must read it. Most importantly the Holy Spirit must reveal the truth of that Word. If you don't know Christ as Lord it is impossible to have the revelation of God's Word. "The letter killeth, but the Spirit giveth life" (2 Corinthians 3:6).

Because my grandfather was murdered, my father is in jail

for murder and I personally aborted two children, I must believe that somewhere in my heritage the door was opened for a spirit of murder to attack my family.

The closer my relationship has grown with Jesus the clearer it has become that there have been spiritual attacks not only on me but my entire family. While studying generational curses I asked God to reveal the curses that had to be broken off of my life.

As He revealed each one to me I began to stand in the authority Christ dying on the cross allows me to have. I applied the blood of Jesus to my life and to my children's lives and began to battle the curses and assignments the devil had launched against my family.

First I stood against the spirit of murder, next the spirits of cancer and infirmity, spirits of addiction, the spirits of lust, pornography and perversion, spirits of anger, spirits of hatred and bitterness, spirits of rejection, isolation, abandonment and persecution. Then finally, the shackles of unforgiveness were broken, giving me the freedom to live life as my heavenly Father had planned for me to live, without bondage and walking in His blessings!

With each revealed spiritual attack confronted and broken off of my life I began to experience freedom and liberty such as I never had before. My mind was clearer, my physical body began to line up with the Word of God and work in perfection. My relationships were healed and reconciliation began to take place.

In Ezekiel 18 the Lord is telling Ezekiel what will happen to the soul that sins. He is also telling the prophet if the son turns away from the sin of the father his righteousness will save him. If you sin there is death. If you turn away from sin you will live. We don't have to be under the curse because of decisions someone else made. We can choose life and turn away from sin. Even though we are all born into sin, because of the fall of Adam, we don't have to live under the curse of sin. Recognizing we have the choice to be free is where liberty begins!

2 Timothy 3:1-7 sums up the generation we are living in perfectly: "This day know also, that in the last days, perilous times shall come. For men shall be lovers of their own selves, covetous, boasters, proud, blasphemers, disobedient to parents, unthankful, unholy, without natural affection, trucebreakers, false accusers, incontinent, fierce, despisers of those that are good. Traitors, heady, high-minded, lovers of pleasures more than lovers of God: Having a form of godliness, but denying the power thereof; from such turn away. For this sort are they which creep into houses, and lead captive silly women laden with sins, led away with divers lusts. Ever learning and never coming to the knowledge of the truth."

The darkness that is beginning to cover the earth from drug abuse, alcoholism, broken homes, sexual abuse, violence, poverty, ignorance, racism, abortion and a meltdown of the family are all symptoms of the larger problem which is a godless society. When God created man He never planned for man to be on his own. His plan was to fellowship with man and to be one with him.

For those of us who have a personal relationship with our heavenly Father it is our responsibility to let others know they have a choice in having a hurtful heritage or a godly one. Mark 16:15 says, "Go ye into all the world and preach the gospel to every creature. He that believeth shall be saved; but he that believeth not shall be damned."

Start right where you are. Ask God to reveal what needs to be broken off of your life. Ask Him to show you the areas you are being held captive by demonic assignments against your life. As you begin to be free share with your family how God is beginning to work in your life. Be ready in and out of season to share the gospel and be prepared to minister to another hurting soul.

How will they know if we don't tell them? That is a very good question. Even though it is hard to believe children aren't being taught to bathe properly or being raised to have common courtesy, it is true. It is also true that here in America there are people that don't know the name of Jesus as anything but a swear word. They don't know we celebrate Jesus' birthday on December 25th. To them it is another holiday with no real meaning behind it.

The only way these things will change is when we as God's children begin to fulfill the Great Commission and tell every living creature the promises of God are true. Learning to walk in the blessings of God is the beginning of true liberty and freedom in Christ Jesus.

I believe one of the first steps in becoming free is breaking generational curses over our own lives and the lives of our children. As generational strongholds are broken, walls will come down that have been preventing entire households from knowing the love of God. The truth of God's Word really will make you free.

In the protection of the Lord you
walk safely today.

David was the apple
Of our Father's eye.
God loved Abraham so much
He sent Isaac by and by
Although God's word does tell us
He loves us all the same
Some seem a little special
When they come in Jesus' name
So I pray that God will bless you
In all you say and do
For our Lord knew you'd be special
When He, in love, created you.

Author Unknown

CHAPTER ELEVEN

An Answer for Today

And be kind to one another, tenderhearted,
forgiving one another, even as God in
Christ forgave you.
Ephesians 4:32

It has been three years since the Lord restored my relationship with my dad and it didn't take long for the enemy to come in with a vengeance in other areas of my life.

Psalm 42 speaks very clearly to define this particular attack. This psalm tells us, "Yea, mine own familiar friend, in whom I trusted, which did eat of my bread, hath lifted up his heel against me." We know the details of how David's relationship with the Lord went wrong and there is great pain in David's cry for help. He feels that he needs to be vindicated.

Usually this is our first reaction to a hurt. The key to this is not putting your expectations on the other person. What we have to remember is that God is working on our behalf and through His Word. He is continually reminding us these times of testing are for us and our well-being. Job 23:10 tells us, "But He knows the way that I take; When He has tested me, I shall come forth as gold."

As God begins to work in our lives, there are seasons of change that we all must go through. These seasons are preparation for the work He has for us.

Kent travels extensively and there have been occasions when we have needed help. Over the years God has provided different individuals as our needs have changed. As I have already mentioned there are seasons in people's lives and while serving Him He prepares you for the tasks He has ahead.

As the seasons in mine and Kent's lives began to change, we knew the seasons would also change for those God sent to help us. We sensed this in our spirits concerning one of the individuals who had served faithfully. We really believed it was time for this person to move in what the Lord was preparing for the future.

For sometime I had felt the season had changed for this individual. Unfortunately, when shared, this escalated into a problem and feelings were hurt. I felt very strongly the way to handle this was in the love of the Lord, hopefully without causing any further anxiety. However, in praying about this the Lord very clearly prepared me that nothing either my husband or myself would convey would be received.

A meeting was arranged and I went into it knowing all I could do was walk in obedience to the Lord and have a loving heart. The encounter did not end as well as we had hoped but we did the best we could do to be obedient to what we felt God had asked of us. The important thing to remember is that even if you don't experience the response you were hoping for, God will respond to your obedience.

Be encouraged that even if you don't experience the fruit when love and forgiveness is extended, you have been obedient to the written Word of God and you have released the other person from how you expect them to react to you. And what's more, you are free from the bondage of unforgiveness in that situation. God looks upon the heart and He knows our weaknesses.

If you are struggling with unforgiveness in a particular area ask Him to give you the faith and the ability to go to that individual. It will set you free. Remember, obedience is always the way to blessing

In my daily devotional, Charles Stanley does a wonderful teaching on the Prodigal Son. In this teaching he states, "making the decision to turn away from sin is the first step toward true freedom. There is no way to enjoy true fellowship with Christ when you are living in sin. Sin separates while obedience unites us in love to God." Even though unforgiveness may not seem like active sin, that is exactly what it is.

In the powerful book, *My Utmost For His Highest*, Oswald Chambers makes the statement there is only one relationship that matters, and that is your personal relationship to a personal God. To maintain the fellowship of a personal relationship with our heavenly Father we must be obedient to His Word. His Word tells us we must forgive others their trespasses so our own trespasses will be forgiven. Throughout the years there have been many opportunities to walk in forgiveness, but after my relationship had been restored with my natural father the Lord gave me such an intense desire to fulfill His Word it really became life to me.

In situation after situation while I was still bound I knew the attacks came from the enemy and I wasn't battling flesh and blood, but spiritual wickedness in high places. Although I was intensely aware the enemy did not want me to walk in freedom it was still hurtful to deal with the rejection over and over again.

What was worse is now I was knowledgeable of God's Word and I knew that in order to walk with Him I must correct any pain that I may have knowingly or unknowingly caused. Have you experienced that? Even though you may not know exactly what the situation is you can feel the urging of the Holy Spirit to go to a friend or a loved one and apologize even though you feel you are the wronged party.

Don't ever think God doesn't know what we need. I love the song, "His Eye Is on the Sparrow." Matthew 10:29 says, "...are not two sparrows sold for a farthing? And one of them shall not fall on the ground apart from your Father's will." Then verses 30 and 31 go on to tell us, "But the very hairs of your head are all numbered. Do not fear therefore; you are of more value than many sparrows." God, through His great faithfulness has proven to me over and over and over again that His eye is on me. Through the many years that I could not call Him Father, He remained ever faithful.

On October 19, 1994 my journal entry begins, "Beverly, you are the apple of my eye." At that time I thought it was very special God would speak that to me and even though I'm sure somewhere in the recesses of my mind I must have known it was in the Bible, it just did not register.

It wasn't until I was sharing it with my dear friend, Lisa Hughes, that it all came together for me. Beyond my wonderful husband and precious family, I consider Lisa a true gift from God. She reached out to me during a time in my life when I really felt I could not go on. Only the Lord could have sent her because as usual, my inner turmoil was kept hidden deep inside of me. But the Lord must have shown her a glimpse of how deep my need was because she appeared just when I needed a real friend most.

Over the years we have spent many happy occasions sitting around her large oak dining room table. We've laughed and cried, complained and rejoiced and solved most of the world's problems while wrapped in the warmth and comfort of our understanding of each other.

After a wonderful meal of Chinese chicken salad and homemade brownies we settled in for a visit. It was, and is, unusual for me to share my journal entries, but I felt comfortable and at ease while I shared what God had been speaking to my heart about being the apple of His eye. During our visit Lisa had mentioned she was reading a tremendous new book by Joyce Meyers entitled, *Tell Them That I Love Them*.

Well, I love Joyce Meyers' teachings and I couldn't wait to look through the little book. As I thumbed through it , the very first page I stopped on, started out, "Joyce, you are the apple of my eye!" You can imagine my surprise because I really had just finished sharing with Lisa how special I felt that the Lord had called me the apple of His eye!

As I continued to read I was amazed to discover like myself, Joyce had not realized this was scripture! I started to get really excited because I knew the Lord was speaking directly to me through His word. The next morning I was at work and Lisa called to tell me she had looked up the scriptures that tell us we are the apple of His eye.

After she shared them with me I got out my study Bible and I learned not only am I the apple of His eye but that as His children we are all considered to be the apple of His eye. In Deuteronomy 32:10 the Word of God tells us, "He found him in a desert land and in the wasteland, a howling wilderness; He encircled him, He instructed him, and He kept him as the apple of His eye."

In verse nine the Word tells us, "For the Lord's portion is His people; Jacob is the place of His inheritance." Jacob is used here as a poetic synonym for Israel. In these two scriptures God is telling Israel He will protect them. Psalm 17:8 says, "Keep me as the apple of Your eye; Hide me under the shadow of Your wings." The phrase concerning the eye is drawn to Deuteronomy 32:10 and refers to sight which is greatly cherished and diligently protected. We know from Psalm 17:8 we are in His sight, we are greatly cherished and He is diligently protecting us.

If you are excited now, hold on, there's more! Proverbs 7:2 tell us, "Keep my commandments and live; and my law as the apple of thine eye." Here the Lord is encouraging us as believers to keep His commandments and trust Him to do His job as a result of our obedience.

Lamentations 2:18 says, "Their heart cried out to the Lord, "O wall of the daughter of Zion, let tears run down like a river day and night; give thyself no rest; let not the apple of thine eye cease." In Proverbs 7:2 the Lord is asking us to keep His law as the apple of our eye but in Lamentations 2:18 He is also letting us know even if we fail and we are judged He will also surely bring restoration if we repent (Leviticus 26:44-45). "Let tears run down," shows us we are not to bottle up our emotions. Tears provide an emotional catharsis for healing.

For those of us who have not been able to cry when a traumatic event has occurred in our lives it is so encouraging to know God provided in His Word an okay for us to let the tears flow. Our healing can truly begin once we have allowed the healing power of God's forgiveness to begin to flow.

Zechariah 2:8 tells us, "For thus saith the Lord of hosts; After the glory He sent me unto the nations which spoiled you, for he that toucheth you toucheth the apple of His eye." To touch the apple of His eye means to stick a finger in the pupil of His eye. Whenever anyone accosts the people of God, it is actually a blasphemous assault against God Himself! That is how much God loves you!

You are the apple of His eye and He wants you to be under His shadow. He wants to protect you and He is so serious about this that any time someone harms you He takes it personally! What a mighty God!

If this is the first time you have ever been told you are the apple of God's eye then I am rejoicing with you because I know what a personal revelation it is—and it is true. God loves you and He wants you to know it.

Let God's amazing grace touch you.

Today

Mend a quarrel.
Search out a forgotten friend,
Dismiss suspicion and replace it with trust.
Write a love letter.
Share some treasure.
Give a soft answer.
Encourage youth.
Manifest your loyalty in a word or deed.
Keep a promise.
Find the time.
Forego a grudge.
Forgive an enemy.
Listen.
Apologize if you were wrong.
Try to understand.
Flout envy.
Examine your demands on others.

Author Unknown

CHAPTER TWELVE

Through a Child's Eyes

*And when He had given thanks, He broke it
and said, "Take, eat; this is My body which is
broken for you; do this in remembrance of Me."*
1 Corinthians 11:24

Today Caleb and I are at the beach with Kent's mom and dad. It is the first time we've been here since Kent's dad, Tom, began his battle with cancer. We are so blessed to be here because we love the condo and the beach but this trip is special because we know the cancer is in remission and God has moved on Tom's behalf.

We have all had many wonderful times here on this beautiful stretch of beach and memories have been made that I will always cherish but today God spoke to me so clearly through an experience with my precious son Caleb.

The beach has always had a special meaning for me and I have worked through many experiences walking up and down the oceanfront on many different beaches. Driving here yesterday I had the time to reflect on my relationship with Kent's parents and how very much I have come to love them and appreciate their influence in my life. My experience with Caleb brought that into sharper focus this morning.

Yesterday it was too windy to go down on the beach so I promised a disappointed seven year old we would head for the beach first thing in the morning if the wind died down.

True to his nature he would not let me forget my promise so promptly at 8:30 a.m. we were headed to the beach.

As usual he was running ahead while I was taking my time and enjoying the absolute beauty of this pristine morning. The beach had been white-washed by the outgoing tide and the shore rose peacefully to meet the incoming waves.

Caleb turned toward me and said, "Look at all the shells, Mom!" I looked but all I saw were broken pieces of shells. He was busily gathering all these broken pieces yelling excitedly for me to come see his treasures. As I walked toward him I said, "Honey, these are all broken, let's look for perfect ones."

He tilted his little head and looked me straight in the eye with those beautiful blue eyes that rivaled the blue sky framing his small form. His expression said it all but he patiently explained that his shells were perfect, couldn't I see all of the colors and the way all the shapes made different patterns?

As I looked at those broken shells held up to me and cupped so lovingly in the palm of those small hands, I did see the beauty of the colors and the patterns that years of being washed over by tons of water had created. As I looked, I knew God was revealing to me the part of Himself that shapes the broken pieces of our lives into a living sacrifice for Him.

There are no perfect lives, only bits and pieces that form the beauty of each individual life. When we allow Him to fit the pieces together we begin to experience the joy of His master plan. As the experiences of life begin to wear on us we can become broken and shattered just as those pieces of shell on the beach had become.

Just as the water flowing over them had created the beautiful patterns and polished the outside to make the colors glow, so will the well of living water that we as Christians are able to draw from wash over us and make our lives whole.

God created us to be whole, not broken. Jesus' broken body was the sacrifice that makes it possible for us to come to our heavenly Father with all of our hurts, wounds, pain and rejection. As we are able to release these to Him He is then able to fit the broken pieces together, allowing our beauty to be uncovered and brought forth.

As I am writing this for you, Caleb is sharing his treasures with his Me-maw and Pop-paw. There are excited oohs and aahs coming from the living room as they share in his discoveries and I can't help but be thankful for what God has put in my own heart.

I have not only been reminded how my heavenly Father has fit the broken pieces of my life back together, but of two of my greatest gifts from Him who are having a wonderful time with their youngest grandson. I am over-whelmed by how blessed I am to be a part of this loving family. Oh Lord, how great Thou art!

You don't have to be perfect to be
loved by others.

The Lord bless you
And keep you
The Lord make His face
To shine upon You
The Lord lift up
His Countenance upon you
And give you peace

Numbers 6:26

CHAPTER THIRTEEN

Wrapped in Love

I remember thee upon my bed and meditate
on You in the night watches.
Psalm 63:6

Last week my husband Kent left for a ten-day trip to Brazil, Costa Rica and Nicaragua. Even though he travels extensively and we are well accustomed to his departures it still takes some time for us to adjust to him being gone again.

The first couple of days are usually the toughest and even though Caleb knows his daddy is called by the Lord to do his job, I still take extra care to make sure he feels a part of what his daddy does. Nights are usually full of home-work, TV time and a lot of encouragement from me for Caleb to settle down and not chase Sassy, our dog, around the house.

However, Caleb was more than a little subdued on this, the second night of his daddy being gone. As we prepared for bed-time I talked to him about his day and we settled down to read stories out of his children's Bible. After story time we turned out the lights for prayer time and instead of going ahead to bed I cuddled up to him for a few extra minutes.

As we lay there I began to really sense the presence of the Lord. Now, at this point let me tell you a little about Caleb's room. It is full of sports items, pinball games, a TV, and lots of toys. But the best part is we have the entire solar system with all of its moons, stars and planets on his ceiling. When you turn out the lights it's like being outside on a clear, crisp evening without a cloud in the sky. As I lay there holding my son in my arms, I began to worship God, singing "Hallelujah." After a few minutes Caleb joined in singing with all his heart. It wasn't too long after that he said, "Mommy, all this singing is making me sleepy," and he laid his head down and went fast asleep. My heart was full of God's love and peace as I lay there under those stars reflecting on the differences between my life as a young child and my children's lives.

Even though their dad is away from home quite often we know he will return and with him will come exciting testimonies of salvation, healings and people walking in freedom. As a child, I too had spent many days and nights waiting for my daddy to return home, but unlike my children I never knew what to expect.

Faith is peace like a child sleeping.

Dear Lord and Father of mankind
Forgive our foolish ways!
Reclothe us in our rightful mind,
In purer lives Thy service find,
In deeper reverence, praise.
Drop Thy still dews of quietness,
Till all our strivings cease;
Take from our souls the strain and stress,
And let our ordered lives confess
The beauty of Thy peace

John Greenleaf Whittier

CHAPTER FOURTEEN

Freedom From Bondage

...Do not be afraid, nor be dismayed, for the
Lord your God is with you wherever you go.
Joshua 1:9

Recently I had the opportunity to share my testimony with a new friend. She has been divorced for four years and was telling me how she felt the Lord had brought her out of Egypt, through the Red Sea, through the wilderness, across the Jordan and now He was leading her on to the Promise Land! I could really relate to what she was sharing because it has not been so very long ago that I counted myself as one of those still in the wilderness rebelling against my heavenly Father.

As she shared her story and we began to exchange life's experiences, I had the most amazing revelation of God's healing power. As we walk through the hurts and pains that all too often occur in our lives, if we are unable to release them, we become bound just like the Israelites were in Egypt, prolonging our wilderness journey.

When Moses came to them and told them he was going to deliver them they were unsure of his leadership and as they crossed out of Egypt they were almost ready to turn back to what was familiar to them. They had a great fear of the unknown and on top of that, Pharaoh's army was really bearing down on them. The pressure must have been tremendous.

Like the Israelites we too would rather hold onto things that are familiar, even if they hurt us. However, at the exact moment the Israelites knew they were going to be caught and killed, God created a miracle that saved them. In their time of need, God parted the Red Sea and allowed them to pass unharmed. So it is with us. At that time God was building their faith. He was proving Himself faithful to what He said He would do. Faith is the key to forgiveness.

Even when God had been faithful to rescue them, the Israelites still hardened their hearts toward God and what, at best, should have been a week's journey ended up being forty years of wandering aimlessly in the wilderness when they could have long since been in the Promise Land enjoying all of that wonderful milk and honey.

Does any of this sound familiar to you? Are you stuck somewhere between Egypt and the Promise Land? God in His infinite mercy forgave the stiff-necked Israelites over and over again bringing them finally, into a place of rest after forty years.

When you continue to hold onto the past it is impossible to walk in the fruits of the Spirit—and that includes walking in liberty and freedom, not being a slave, bound by circumstances that are beyond your control. What's more, when we don't have the faith to forgive, God will give that to us as well. All we have to do is ask. It is that simple.

Okay, so for some of us it may not be easy to ask the Lord to help us. That was the biggest step for me. I wanted to trust my heavenly Father but I didn't know how to get there. My friend, that is my whole purpose in writing this book. If nothing else you read between the covers of this book ministers to you, it is my prayer that this gets straight into your spirit.

If you are struggling in your relationship with God, don't let go! In looking over your life you can see the evidence of God's plan for you. The choices you made may not have been His will for you but He was always there waiting for you to turn to Him.

My pastor preached a powerful message on Jacob wrestling with God and he said something I will never forget. He said if you don't wrestle with God you will wrestle with man.

My whole life had been spent wrestling with man and in that moment I made a vow to God that I would not let go of Him. In that service my heart began to melt toward my heavenly Father and for the first time I realized how bound I was by unforgiveness and rejection.

God allowed me to see that to overcome rejection I must begin to walk in forgiveness. That was on February 21, 1993, exactly six years to the day that we had moved to Florida. Six is the number of man and as I listened to the message I knew God was setting me free from the fear of man and was bringing me out of bondage to my past.

I had been trying to know God without having a relationship with Him. The same emptiness that had dominated my relationship with my natural father had prevented me from knowing the fulfillment of a relationship with my heavenly Father.

Without fellowship it was impossible to call Him Father. There is no relationship without fellowship. The Word of God says in Exodus 20:12 to honor thy father and thy mother. I was not honoring my natural father in any way and that caused an even deeper breach between God and myself.

Once my heart softened toward my heavenly Father His Holy Spirit began to work in me, but it still took time and testing before I was able to walk in true obedience to what God commands us to do. This was the beginning of deliverance for me and in big bold letters at the top of my journal is written, "THIS MESSAGE CHANGED MY LIFE!"

From that day on I came to know my God as Abba, Father and with that revelation has come freedom and peace such as I have never known before.

*God will heal every hurt in
your heart.*

The world is a great mirror.
It reflects back to you what you are.
If you are loving, if you are friendly, if you are helpful,
The world will prove loving and friendly and helpful to you.
The world is what you are.

Thomas Dreier

CHAPTER FIFTEEN

Seeking God's Answers

For the Son of Man came to seek and to
save that which was lost.
Luke 19:10

This summer I spent ten days in my hometown. In the entire eleven years since I moved away, this was my longest visit and I had looked forward to it for several months.

Since communication started between my father and myself, a new openness has developed between me and my sisters and brother. Because I left home at such an early age there aren't a lot of shared experiences between all of us as a family.

We all have individual, one-on-one things that have happened but not a lot of growing up experiences in common. This is especially true of my brother who was only a baby when I left. As adults we are all working diligently to create bonds between us that were never developed as children.

Since I have become a Christian my hope to see all of my family saved has played a very important role in each of our relationships. The Lord showed me that the only way I could be an effective witness for my family was to do it by example and let them see the change in me. There have been so many times I have grown impatient.

Even though I have experienced many struggles as a Christian, I have the knowledge that Jesus Christ is the rock my faith is built upon. I can trust Him to work through any situation. When you know God is always working on your behalf and you want so much for those you love to have that same confidence it is very difficult to not try to hurry up the process.

I found this to be true as I encountered old friends from my past that had heard I was a Christian and a pastor's wife. They were very curious about the changes in my life as long as I didn't try to convert them or impose any of my beliefs on them.

Time after time I was asked how I could stand to give up all of the fun things in life and lead such a boring Christian existence. The only answer I had for them was that serving God was the most exciting thing I had ever experienced. Then I explained to them that God isn't some big judgmental entity sitting in heaven waiting for you to screw up so He can blast you. He is the God that thousands of years ago decided He was lonely so He created man in His image to have someone to hang out with. God is the God of partying.

For the most part everyone I shared this with said, "Really?!" But through that witness, I have seen many hearts softened toward a loving God. All they had heard of Him was that you have to give up everything that you enjoyed and wear ugly clothes and go without. I have to confess that was my understanding of Christianity until Jesus came to live in my heart.

This interpretation is man's and the point was brought home

to me on this same trip. For the past year my dear friends Debbie and Hal Gray have opened their home to me so I would have a place to stay when I visit my father. Debbie and I have been friends practically since birth and we are really enjoying renewing our relationship. She has always had a green thumb and every home she has lived in, she has brightened with annuals and all sorts of gorgeous trees.

Every morning that I am there we always sit on her front porch swing and enjoy a cup of coffee. On my last day there our conversation turned to the Bible. As usual she had a lot of questions for me. The main concern seemed to be how could we, in 1995, count on the Bible to be accurate, because after all, it is just a historical account, interpreted by men?

I explained to her the best way I could that the Bible is in fact a historical account of bygone days. But, the Bible is also the Spirit of God in written form and the men who were used of God were led by the Spirit of God in writing it.

I went on to explain, yes, there have been translations from the Hebrew and the Greek in which the Bible was originally written. As we grow in our knowledge of the Word of God, He reveals to us, by His Spirit, how to use the many resources that are available to us, so we will know what the Bible means, to us as God's children today.

2 Timothy 3:16-17 says, " All scripture is given by inspiration of God, and is profitable for doctrine, for reproof, for correction, for instruction in righteousness; that the man of God may be perfect, thoroughly furnished unto all good works." The sad part was I knew that until God reveals this to her and others by His Spirit, they will never understand because "the letter killeth but the Spirit giveth life" (2 Corinthians 3:6).

In trying to be a witness for Christ by example and letting my lifestyle speak for itself, one of the most effective tools has been the forgiveness for my father that has occurred in my whole family. Those who have known of my estrangement and the reasons for it are full of questions of how it came about and what initiated the first visit. Because of this I have had many open doors to witness and to share what Jesus did for me when He came to live in my heart.

The hardest part of sowing is waiting for the harvest, and I can tell you I would not have made a very good farmer. As I was praying about all my family members receiving salvation, and watching them still going through so much hurt and turmoil, I was reminded of the parable of the five foolish virgins and the five wise virgins in Matthew chapter 25:1-14.

The parable tells us that while the bridegroom slept, five of the ten prepared themselves for the wedding feast and five of them did not. When the time came for the appearing of the bridegroom the foolish virgins wanted the supplies the wise virgins had prepared and when they wouldn't share, they had to run out and stock up.

By the time they got back, the wedding had taken place and the door was shut. In verses 11 and 12 it says, "Afterward came also the other virgins, saying Lord, Lord open to us. But he answered and said, I know you not."

Like you, I don't want this to happen to my loved ones. Unfortunately, in today's society, the decision to accept Christ doesn't become a priority until we are on our way out of this world — not while we are still contending with all the strife connected to living in the ninties. Everyone just goes about their day-to-day living without giving a thought to where they will spend eternity.

My question to you is how will they know if we don't tell them? It is our job to do so. We are commissioned to spread the gospel to those who have not heard it and to pray for those who have and have not made that decision to serve God.

I delayed in writing this book because I wanted it to have a happy ending. I wanted my father to be saved and serving God with all his heart. To my knowledge he has not made a public confession of his faith, but I know there is a difference in his life, and I know that difference is Christ.

My part was to be obedient to God and forgive him. The rest is between him and God. In the meantime I will continue to pray for him and all of the people I know and love that have not made that life-changing choice. I encourage you to do the same.

In your witness to others it is so important to do as writer Tony Campolo suggests and contextualize the gospel so it fits with the person and the setting you are working with and within. In his book, *The Kingdom of God Is a Party*, he shares how to express the very essence of what I believe Christ came to convey to sinners; once we are reconciled to God through the blood of Jesus Christ, there is a party waiting for us that ear hath not heard nor eye seen. That party is the kingdom of God.

In preparing to write this book, my goal was to reach unsaved individuals that did not feel comfortable in a church setting and were perhaps coming out of a lifestyle or circumstance that was so painful they felt as though there was no chance of any church ever accepting them. I have experienced that sense of rejection and I can tell you it is one of Satan's best tools to keep someone bound. There are few things worse than being afraid that God will reject you. It is heartbreaking but there are countless thousands of people struggling with that right now.

After much prayer I have come to the understanding that the teaching of forgiveness is much needed in the body of Christ as well. Healing needs to take place throughout the entire body so we can accomplish what God has asked each one of us to do for His kingdom. If our body is physically depleted we can not perform physical tasks. The same is true of our spirit life.

If there are areas where you are being hindered by the attacks of the enemy, you need to be healed in that area so you can be the most effective witness for Christ you can be.

I pray that by sharing how God healed me, you too, will experience the same healing power in the area you need it most.

There is hope everlasting.

Love suffereth long and is kind,
Love envieth not, love vaunteth not itself,
Is not puffed up, doth not behave itself unseemly,
Seeketh not its own, is not provoked,
Taketh not account of evil,
Rejoiceth not in unrighteousness,
But rejoiceth with the truth;
Beareth all things, believeth all things,
Hopeth all things, endureth all things,
Love never faileth.

   1 Corinthians 13 (ASV)

CHAPTER SIXTEEN

Life Lessons

He also brought me up out of a horrible pit,
out of the miry clay, And set my feet upon
a rock, and established my steps.
Psalm 40:2

Our oldest son, Josh, is a tall, handsome young man. He has an outgoing personality and from the time he could express an opinion, he's been very conservative. He thinks everything through and weighs the circumstances. Like the rest of us, sometimes temptation has presided over common sense, but for the most part he has used wisdom beyond his years and managed to make good choices, if not always the ones I would have made for him.

I have credited Josh with saving my life because if I had not become a mother when I did, my life would have gone in a completely different direction. Josh brought meaning to my life and gave me worth. He has always been a tremendous source of joy and because there are only 18 years difference in our ages he has been a friend to me as well as a son. If anyone really knows me as a person, it's Josh. I have counted on him to be strong and to trust me even if the decisions I made did not make much sense to him. He has always been very practical and down to earth whereas, I have not.

Imagine my surprise when I received a telephone call late one evening and it was Josh on the line telling me this big, long story of how he and his best friend had decided to take his pride and joy, an Isuzu Amigo truck, four-wheeling.

My first reaction was to point out to him the Amigo is not a four-wheel drive. He told me he knew that but the area they were driving in had seemed harmless enough at first with just the tires getting wet. They had been having a great time weaving in and out of the mud and water when all of a sudden the depth of the water went from being mid-tire to being cab deep. Another vehicle had apparently gotten stuck and in trying to work its way out it had dug a really big hole.

As my son sat there in the murky water he knew his truck was really stuck. They both climbed out and pushed but to no avail. As he was telling me the story he shuddered as he relayed what it felt like standing in waist deep water with unknown creatures going past his legs. The worst part was the truck was really sunk and it was too late to get a tow truck out to the site.

Kent was out of town and Josh was really afraid that when he came home he would be angry. We were paying for the insurance on the truck and Josh was concerned that even though we had full coverage it would not pay for a sunk truck.

Little did we know at the time that leaving the truck over night would ruin the computer system for the whole truck and that before it would run again the entire computer system, the clutch and the engine would be replaced.

Because Kent has been Josh's daddy since he was nine years old their relationship has grown through many experiences. They love one another and they have mutual respect for one another, but all I could hear in my twenty year old son's voice was the fear he had failed and his daddy was going to be disappointed in him.

How many times have we been in this same situation? It seems to be just a little thing but deep within our very being we know it for what it truly is. We may think we're just getting toe deep into sin but before we know what hit us we are neck deep into flood waters and we can see no way out.

The Holy Spirit warned us but we went ahead and made the choice to hold onto our anger, hold that grudge, let bitter words pour hotly onto a loved one or whatever it was you made the choice to do. God knows that we are going to make the wrong choices

In her book, *Pack Up Your Gloomies in a Great Big Box*, Barbara Johnson puts it this way: "Did you ever think of your life with all the mistakes and sins of the past, as being much like the tangles in a ball of yarn?... It's a comfort to know we can get up and face each day by putting ourselves and our loved ones in His loving hands, knowing that in His loving mercy He will untangle it all."

God's loving mercy is too incredible for our intellect to grasp. That is why we must be born again of the Spirit. We will never be able to understand God's mercy and grace as an unbeliever. John 3:5 states, "...unless a man be born of water and of the Spirit, he cannot enter into the kingdom of God. The Spirit refers to the spiritual birth brought about by the renewing and transforming power of the Holy Spirit.

Without this renewing of our mind and spirit through the Holy Spirit we will never have a true understanding of how God's mercy and grace works in us, ever shaping us in His image.

Regardless of our past mistakes, present mistakes and future mistakes once we experience the redemptive power of being born again we begin to walk in God's infinite mercy.

Any time you are reminded of mistakes you have made, remember, God has forgiven you. He will never remind you of the past. Only the accuser brings up the past. Our heavenly Father's mercies are new every morning and once we are forgiven He shows us how to look to the future as He does.

Only God knows the plan He has for our lives, but Satan knows he can keep us bound to our past if we are continually looking back, punishing ourselves, instead of looking forward and walking in the freedom forgiveness brings.

Because my relationship with my own parents was such a mess I made the decision to never let that happen in my own family. Kent and I were not saved when he first became Josh's daddy and we did a lot of things in our personal lives that were destroying us, but where Josh was concerned, he was our number one priority.

He was the center of our lives and when Caleb was born we wanted both of our children to know they were the most important part of our lives. We were saved right before I became pregnant with Caleb and from the very beginning he has been prayed over and has never known life without Jesus being the main focus of our family.

Our desire as parents has been to reflect as much of God as we can. We have sincerely tried to present godly characteristics that reflect the presence of God in our own lives. Ephesians 4:23 says, "And be renewed in the spirit of your mind." It is a continual process and it is a decision we must make every moment before we speak or take action in any given situation.

There are always going to be opportunities to make the wrong choice but if we have made the one choice that is the most important, accepting Jesus Christ as Lord and Savior, our heavenly Father has provided, in His love letter to us—the Bible—every answer we need for Christian growth. And the most incredible thing is He knows we will continue to make mistakes but He will continue to be merciful and forgive us because as His children we walk in His grace.

It was three long months before Josh's truck was back on the road. His fear of failure was unfounded and we did everything we could to help him while he was truckless. My husband was very supportive and my son is forever grateful. After all we have been through as a family the most important thing comes down to knowing how to be supportive of one another.

I thank God for healing me so I can be the mother God intended me to be, loving, supportive and godly. Like the rest of the human race I will continue to make mistakes and there will be defeats but I know beyond a shadow of a doubt that nothing I will ever do will separate me from the love of God (Romans 8:35). You too can have that assurance.

Don't let the mud of sin prevent you from knowing Christ as your Lord and Savior. Revelation 1:5 says, "...Jesus Christ...that loved us... washed us from our sins in His own blood." That's how much He loves you.

For years I didn't think I could ever be loved by God or be forgiven of my sins. If you think your past or present is stopping God from loving you, remember, when we deserve it least, He loves us most and once we have made the decision to serve Him, tribulation or distress or persecution or famine or nakedness or peril or sword will not separate us from the love of God.

*Be confident God has a plan when trials
and suffering are causing discouragement.*

The Spirit itself beareth witness with our spirit,
that we are the children of God;
And if children, then heirs;
Heirs of God, and joint heirs with Christ;
If so be that we suffer with Him,
That we may also be glorified together.

Romans 8:16-17

CHAPTER SEVENTEEN

Heart of the Home

For I am the Lord, I do not change.
Malachi 3:6

It is 7:45 a.m. and we are all rushing around the house playing beat the clock. If the boys don't leave at exactly 8:00 a.m. they will be late, Josh for work and Caleb for school.

Monday mornings are usually the only mornings my husband is at home so he likes to be a part of the morning ritual. The problem is we have a very small galley kitchen that opens into a combination dining area and den. In the midst of everyone preparing for their days I am in the middle of the chaos making sure everything they need is accessible to them. A galley kitchen is really a lot like the kitchen on a boat in that everything can be reached from the center.

It is limited space at best but when you have a family of four plus the dog running circles around your ankles it can become very frustrating. Kent's favorite place to stand is right in front of the coffeemaker. This gives him a great observation point but it is also right in my way.

It used to drive me wild having all of them crowding around me until I realized it wasn't limited to our early morning hectic pace. What ever room I am in, my family slowly gravitates to that part of the house. When we come to the end of a busy day we each head to our private space but it is just a matter of time before we have all settled down in the same room for television watching or just a visit to catch up on one another's day.

Another interesting item I have noted is that my mood sets the tone for the whole household. If I am happy and content then the mood is light and fun. If I'm tired and testy then my family becomes quiet and withdrawn, waiting and watching for my reactions to them. If, for whatever reason I lose my temper and they retreat from my anger it is only a matter of time before they cautiously test the waters of parental or wifely-shortcomings and once again gather around.

The realization that I am truly the heart of the home has on occasion filled me with such pure joy that tears of love and appreciation pour down my face. My family is able to over-look my failures because we have a relationship. They are drawn to me time and time again because the foundation has been laid over many years.

They love me unconditionally—imperfections and all. If I am having a bad day they don't reject me or my love. They know that my mood will pass and that no matter how angry or busy I am they can come to me and I will, to the best of my ability, meet their needs and soothe and comfort them.

Knowing my children and my husband love me and accept me for who I am is a great source of strength to me. Knowing that even when I fail and make a mess of things they will always support me, gives me a strong sense of belonging. But without my heavenly Father's unconditional love I would not be walking in the fullness of what He has given me.

God has honored me by giving me the gift of being a wife and mother. He has entrusted me to train two beautiful sons to know Him as Lord and Savior. God treasures me. I don't have to be perfect to serve Him. He knows my imperfections and loves me because of them.

When I have made a mistake I don't have to be in fear He will turn His back on me. He is always there for me and for you. God is our refuge and strength and a very present help in the time of trouble (Psalm 46:1-2). Just as my children come to me, so we can go to our heavenly Father. Unlike me, He is not moody. His precepts do not change. He is the same yesterday, today and forever. He wants us to come to Him and lay down those heavy burdens we have been carrying around.

My favorite time of night is right before we are getting ready to head to our separate rooms. Josh usually comes in and drapes himself across the foot of the bed and shares his heart with me.

Without fail, Caleb and Sassy come running in to make sure they aren't missing out on anything fun. We laugh and cut-up, the boys wrestle, then I send them off to bed. No matter how long the day has been it is always a time of refreshing for me.

My children seek me out as the heart of our home. I bring continuity, support, understanding and above all, unconditional love. If I, an earthly vessel can be filled with all of these strengths for my children, how much more does our heavenly Father desire to reveal Himself to you as the heart of your very being?

You don't have to test the waters of godly love. Once we have a relationship with God He readily accepts us, failures and all. We are His children, and He may chastise us. When we are truly yielded to the Spirit of God He treats us like His children. Hebrews 12:5-6 says "...My son, despise not thou the chastening of the Lord, nor faint when thou are rebuked of Him; for whom the Lord loveth He chasteneth, and scourgeth every son whom He receiveth." Verse 7 goes on to say, "If ye endure chastening, God dealeth with you as with sons; for what son is he whom the father chasteneth not?"

Just like my boys know that when they are disciplined for misbehaving I am loving them because they are being chastised, so God chastises and scourges us of sin. My boys know that when the discipline has passed, our relationship will continue in an attitude of forgiveness and repentance. They won't have to earn sonship because it is their inheritance and that right is an unearned benefit to being born into this family.

In Pastor Benny Hinn's book, *Welcome Holy Spirit*, there is a passage that addresses the spirit of sonship. He uses Galatians 4:6-7, "And because you are sons, God has sent forth the spirit of His son into your hearts, crying Abba, Father. Therefore you are no longer a slave but a son, and if a son, then an heir of God through Christ."

We don't have to earn sonship either. We have been adopted into the family of God. Romans 8:15-17 makes this clear, "...ye have received the spirit of adoption...the Spirit itself beareth witness with our spirit, that we are the children of God; and if children, then heirs; heirs of God, and joint heirs with Christ..."

If then we are the children of the living God can we not go to Him, just as we would a loving parent? The answer is yes. Romans 8:14-15 tells us, "For as many as are led by the Spirit of God, they are the sons of God. For ye have not received the spirit of bondage again to fear..." We must have the fear of the Lord that comes from respect for who He is, but I believe above all else He wants us to be able to come to Him as little children come to a loving parent. He wants us to be drawn to Him because He is our loving, heavenly Father. In the middle of the day-to-day chaos that is in our lives, invite Him into your hearts and homes to bring order.

Let Him set the tone for your everyday living. He is there waiting and watching for you. He has prepared a feast for you and through His Word you can dine with Him. Just like I call my children in for suppertime, so He is calling to you to **come, dine, fellowship**. Take the time to develop the relationship and know Him as Father. His arms are open wide, ready to embrace you.

Don't look to God as the stern taskmaster who demands our obedience, but as the loving Father who wins it.

Are not five sparrows sold
For two farthings, and not one
Of them is forgotten before God?
But even the very hairs
Of your head are numbered.
Fear not therefore; ye are of
More value than many sparrows.

Luke 12:6-7

CHAPTER EIGHTEEN

More of Christ, Less of Me

*He must increase, but I must decrease. (He must
grow more prominent; I must grow less so.)
John 3:30*

We have a houseguest. For the past week I have been
watching two sparrows build a nest in one of my houseplants
on our back porch. They fly in and out the wide open screen
door. I wanted to keep the door closed but Sassy has a habit
of having nocturnal potty adventures so I keep the door open
so she can run right out without me having to walk onto the
back porch.

After several days of watching the busy parents I decided
to check on their progress and was delighted to see five little
eggs in the nest! For two mornings I tiptoed out to see if the
mother was on the eggs trying to determine when would be
the best time to show the eggs to Caleb. Friday morning I
checked again and there was no sign of the mother so I fig-

ured she must hunt for food at night and sit on the eggs during the day.

I hurriedly got Caleb up and he rode piggy-back out to see the eggs telling him I had a big surprise for him. We went out the door and headed straight for the plant. I told him to get ready and to look real hard and to tell me what he saw. By this time we were right over the nest and I peered down and looked straight into the eyes of the little momma sparrow!

I don't know who was more surprised, the bird, Caleb or me. The chain reaction that followed was this: the bird immediately hid her head under her wing, making her look for the world like a little brown cottonball, I took off running and Caleb held on for dear life hollering, "Why are you running? I didn't see anything!"

I wasn't sure why I was running but it sure was funny. I was so surprised to see the momma bird there I just took off. Of course, now Caleb knew there were bird eggs on our back porch and he was asking a million questions. "How many eggs are there Mommy?" "When can I see them?" "Why couldn't I see the mommy bird?" "Were you scared of the bird?" "Mommy, is there a daddy bird?" "Where is the daddy bird?" It was all I could do to get him ready for school. His last question was "Can I please see the eggs when I get home?" Then he ran out the door.

As I stood there watching the nest I realized the plant would probably die because I wouldn't be able to water it. In that moment that plant began to symbolize my own walk with Christ. My daily prayer is that there will be less of me and more of Him. Daily I ask that more of my flesh will die so more of my spirit will live. If I water the plant then I'll ruin the nest and the eggs' protection would be gone. They may survive but will they be as healthy and strong?

As I thought this over I remembered the mother bird's reaction to me. She hid her head under her wing as soon as she saw me. I must have seemed like a giant to her. Even though my intentions were to protect her and her little nest she didn't know that.

That is so like us humans. In my relationship with the Lord it took a long time to understand that by submitting to His authority I was coming under His protection. My first revelation of this was the way I related to my husband.

When Kent and I were first together I was very independent. The world's expectations are based on how much you achieve and your level of worth is measured by your success. Kent was very successful at the beginning of our relationship but there came a time when he could not meet any of our needs. As we struggled to get back on our feet I experienced the same distrust in his ability to protect me and provide for me that I had as a little girl toward my father. When we were first saved I could not get past the teaching on submission in the church.

Ephesians 5:22-23 tells us, "Wives, submit yourselves unto your own husband, as unto the Lord. For the husband is the head of the wife, even as Christ is the head of the church; and He is the Saviour of the body." I simply could not trust Kent to take care of me.

I finally came to the understanding that I was putting a tremendous amount of pressure on Kent to do something only God can do. Yes, Kent was my husband and our provider but I was expecting him to meet all of my emotional needs as well as my spiritual ones, but I wasn't doing anything to help. I was still trying to do everything in my life in my own strength.

In the book, *When the Glass Slipper Doesn't Fit and the Silver Spoon Is in Someone Else's Mouth*, Claire Cloninger sums it up like this. "I went from my old routine of dancing for the approval of the world to dancing for the approval of God and His people." That is exactly how I began to behave.

I didn't know how to submit to God's authority and I certainly didn't realize it was for my own protection. It was a lot like being caught in a torrential downpour and saying no, thank-you, just keep that big umbrella all to yourself, I can make it without it.

That doesn't make much sense, does it? But when we reject God's outstretched hand that is exactly what we do. We walk away from His covering and His protection. Just like the little sparrow hiding her head under her wing we think we become invisible to God if we just pretend He isn't there.

I ran from God's protection for a whole litany of reasons, but the bottom line was I didn't trust Him. I thought of God as a big, angry entity, waiting for me to make a mistake so He could judge me and punish me. Because of that perception I COULD NOT CALL HIM FATHER. I could not accept His protection. I could not submit my life to Him.

Believe it or not, it was actually because of my hardness that I was finally able to accept God's protection. Over the years my exterior had become so glossed over it was like having shellac as an outer covering. With each perceived hurt, wound or rejection, another coat of shellac would go on and one more layer of Bev would disappear. Finally, the surface simply began to crack.

The pressures of being in the public eye and being a pastor's wife began to take its toll. I was leading a dual life and not doing it well. God wanted my all and I was unable to give it.

I will never forget the morning I sat down with my husband and told him I needed counseling because I felt like I was losing my mind. Actually, my veneer was cracking. The shellac was beginning to crack, but I didn't know that.

My journal entry that morning, February 1, 1991 reads, "I ask you once again to hear my cries and fill my heart with your love and mercy and grace. So many times I have said my old man has come off in layers and it still is." The scripture the Lord took me to was, "I will receive you and will be a Father unto you and ye shall be my ...daughter, saith the Lord Almighty" (2 Corinthians 6:17-18).

It took me another year to really hear what the Lord was telling me. He had already received me as His daughter! That morning was a turning point in my acceptance of my husband as my covering though. He heard me out and told me I wasn't losing my mind but I was over extended and it was time to evaluate my priorities. There were some things I needed to be less involved in and he would help me make those decisions and he would support me in whatever I decided to do. Then he gently reminded me that as my covering it was his responsibility to protect me.

As a result of my acceptance of submission as protection God began to reveal more and more of His nature to me. I was able to turn in my cracked surface for the whole armor of God and what had seemed like a sacrifice that would make me a doormat literally became the key that opened the door to my healing.

My houseguest is sitting protectively on her eggs. The plant is a sacrifice I willingly make. I wish it was that easy to make sacrifices in all areas of our life. Even though it is hard to sacrifice the things that please our flesh it is very encouraging to know that the more of us that goes, the more Christ is within us. No matter what the sacrifice, that makes it worthwhile.

Where there is faith, God's voice
calls for me to keep walking.

When the Holy Spirit controls our lives
He will produce this kind of fruit in us:
Love, joy, peace, patience, kindness, goodness,
Faithfulness, gentleness and self-control.

Galatians 5:22-23

CHAPTER NINETEEN

The New Me

*...but one thing I do, forgetting those things which
are behind and reaching forward to those things
which are ahead, I press toward the goal for the
prize of the upward call of God in Christ Jesus.*
Philippians 3:13-14

Last Sunday I was sitting in church really enjoying the
teaching when our pastor had us turn to Genesis 18. This passage of scripture demonstrates God's decision to destroy the
city of Sodom. Abraham had reasoned with Him, pleaded with
Him and even tried to strike up a deal.

The problem was the people in Sodom did not want to be
delivered from their wicked ways. They liked their lifestyle
and it had obviously never occurred to them that life without
their fleshly desires would ultimately bring them into God's
kingdom and eternal life.

Little did Lot realize as he packed up his own family that they would also struggle in making the choice to leave. He might have thought his family was happy to be rescued from the destruction the angels had warned him about. Even though it is Lot doing the asking about their destination, there are reasons to believe his wife may have been behind them!

Genesis 18:17-20 states: "And it came to pass, when they had brought them forth abroad, that he said, 'Escape for thy life; look not behind thee, neither stay thou in all the plain; escape to the mountain lest thou be consumed.' And Lot said unto them, 'Oh not so, my Lord; behold now, thy servant hath found grace in thy sight and thou hast magnified thy mercy, which thou has shewed unto me in saving my life; and I cannot escape to the mountain, lest some evil take me and I die; behold now this city is near to flee unto, and it is a little one; Oh, let me escape thither, (is it not a little one) and my soul shall live."

Lot and his family have just been saved from utter destruction and he is concerned about his soul not living in a city. We don't know a lot about Lot's wife but it seems that city living suited her way of life. Lot's concern to remain a city dweller most likely stemmed from his desire to continue to provide the type of life his wife and daughters had come to expect.

Mrs. Lot probably had not been involved in the decision-making process when the angels were hurrying Lot to depart from the city. Mrs. Lot was hanging onto her past. The angels of the Lord told them very specifically, "...look not behind thee" (Genesis 18:17), but as the Lord's wrath poured down on Sodom, Lot's wife looked back from behind him, and she became a pillar of salt (Genesis 18:26). I have always wondered why God chose salt.

My Spirit-Filled Bible gives the explanation that a pillar of salt was likely chosen since salt was the major trade of the area. Judgment engulfed her because her affections were with Sodom and not God. She just could not let go of her past. Even though we know from scripture that the city of Sodom was full of perversion, violence and enough sin to provoke the Lord to destroy it, Genesis 18:20 tells us, "their sin is very grievous," still she could not release it.

Because she could not let go, God could not begin to reveal Himself to her. Her whole family had been rescued because of Abraham's petition before God. 2 Peter 2:7-8 says, "And the Lord delivered just Lot, vexed with the filthy conversation of the wicked; For that righteous man dwelling among them, in seeing and hearing, vexed his righteous soul from day to day with their unlawful deeds..."

Even though Lot was found to be righteous, there were not ten righteous men to be found so God chose to deliver Lot for the sake of his uncle. This miracle went right over Mrs. Lot's head.

When we hold onto the bondages of our past, we are not unlike Mrs. Lot. She allowed her desire to hold onto the past, control her future and became a symbol of disobedience for all eternity. When we are continually looking back and reliving our pain and suffering that occurred years ago the Holy Spirit can not complete His work in our spirits to create the new man.

Once we have experienced the incredible miracle of salvation the next step is to "...put off the old man with his deeds; and ...put on the new man, which is renewed in knowledge after the image of Him that created him" (Colossians 3:9-10).

Shortly before my husband and I entered the ministry Kent came home one night in a terrible state of mind. For months he had battled a spirit of fear and on this particular evening he told me he couldn't stand the confusion that was attacking his mind any longer. The fear inside of him was beginning to overwhelm him and he simply could not think clearly.

I didn't really understand what he was experiencing and I did not have a lot of biblical training or expertise in battling spiritual attacks, but God gave me revelation knowledge that because Kent had made the choice to serve Him, the old man and all of its encumbrances were being put off, and with the new man was coming the mind of Christ.

Kent was in effect losing his old mentality and the ways of the past and beginning to walk in the knowledge of Christ. From that night on he was never attacked by the spirit of fear or confusion!

Kent made the choice to be free of his past. It took me much longer to come to the understanding that the Holy Ghost was being hindered by me hanging onto my past. Believe me, it wasn't that I wanted to be stuck in all of those painful memories, I wanted them to conform to the new me I had created.

Romans 12 tells us, "and be not conformed to this world; but be ye transformed by the renewing of your mind, that ye may prove what is that good and acceptable, and perfect will of God." I left out that perfect will of God part and embarked on a futile journey to renew, restore and replace events that had occurred that just didn't fit in with my new image.

This is an impossible task! Just like the areas in your life that you haven't dealt with and are too painful for your mind to touch on, mine were always lurking in corners just waiting for me to trip over them.

One of the biggest obstacles we run into—not just as believers—but as human beings is the desire to be vindicated. So often instead of letting go of the problem and allowing God to work we want to rehash every little detail of how we have been hurt. It seems to ease the pain when we surround ourselves with folks that are eager to relive each blow-by-blow account of the "somebody done me wrong" song that we are continually singing.

In fact, if all we are doing is reliving the pain while still holding onto it, we are not only destroying our chances for deliverance and healing, but every time the hurt is shared with someone new the burden of knowledge now rests on their shoulders as well. The pain you have been carrying is transferred to each person you have shared it with.

In the Philippians 4:8, Paul encourages the Philippians to practice purity and the peace of God in this manner; "Finally, brethren, whatsoever things are true, whatsoever things honest, whatsoever things are just, whatsoever things are pure, whatsoever things are lovely, whatsoever things are of good report; if there be any virtue, and if there be any praise, think on these things." Verse 9 goes on to say, "Those things which ye have learned, and received, and heard, and seen in me, do; and the peace of God shall be with you."

I realize how very difficult it is to always think about things that are true, honest, just, pure, lovely, of good report, virtuous or full of praise. Especially, if you are just coming out of a situation that may have taken years to even talk about.

That is why it is absolutely imperative that we come to our Father God with our hurts, wounds and needs. We can talk about our hurts over and over again but if we don't come to the cross daily we continue in our hurt without the hope that was given to us by Christ dying on the cross. We are literally rejecting the greatest gift He has ever given us.

God redeemed us through the blood of Jesus Christ, forgave our sins and adopted us as His sons and daughters, freeing us from the bondage of the world, including all of the pain inflicted by the world. In giving us the liberty to bring our daily burdens and problems straight to Him in prayer, He gave us hope eternal that whatever situation we are walking in or through or out of He is the one carrying the load for us.

Galatians 4:3-7 demonstrates this clearly; "Even so we...were in bondage under the elements of the world; but when the fullness of the time was come, God sent forth His Son...to redeem them that were under the law, that we might receive the adoption of sons. And because ye are sons, God hath sent forth the spirit of His Son into your hearts, crying Abba, Father. Wherefore thou art no more a servant, but a son; and if a son, then an heir of God through Christ."

If we don't come to our heavenly Father daily, laying personal anguish at His feet, we continue to carry all of our problems in our own strength. This is not God's intention nor His perfect will for our lives.

It is a choice we make to keep the lines of communication open between ourselves and God when we come daily to the throne of God in prayer. Our minds must be purged daily of the pollution that comes from day-to-day living. Just like pollution clouds our environment so does the lack of communing with God cloud our focus.

Day in and day out we are continually working out the issues of day-to-day living. When we are in constant communion with the Holy Spirit we are at peace. Romans 8:6 confirms the mind controlled by the Holy Spirit is life and peace. 1 Corinthians 13:13 says, "there are three things that remain, faith, hope and love—the greatest of these is love."

1. Faith is the foundation and content of God's message.

2. Hope is the attitude and focus.

3. Love is the action.

When faith and hope are in line you are free to love truly because you understand how God loved. Loving others is the key to being like Christ!

God is all the hope we need. He promises to be a shield to protect us. When we focus our thoughts on God our hope is restored. Don't wait for events to make you feel helpless. Stay focused on your relationship with God for He is your only help.

Satan, not God wants us to suffer. If we are hopeless instead of hopeful, joyless instead of joyful, helpless instead of helpful, then our focus stays where our problems are. We must never lose sight of who it is that wants us to suffer. Our enemy knows suffering often destroys our faith in God and kills our hope.

In 1 Peter 5:8-9 Peter instructs believers to be alert so in the midst of their suffering they will know where the adversity is coming from as well as how God is going to use it to strengthen their faith in Him. "Be sober, be vigilant; because your adversary the devil, as a roaring lion, walketh about, seeking whom he may devour; whom resist steadfast in the faith, knowing that the same afflictions are accomplished in your brethren that are in the world."

It is our job to share this hope with others. In the beginning of this chapter we saw Lot's wife turned into a pillar of salt for her disobedience. I want to encourage you to be obedient to God's Word and let go of those burdens that have been so hard to let go of.

In Matthew 28:20 the Lord says, "I am with you always, even unto the end of the world." That is the very reason we have this precious gift of hope, we know He is with us always. God wants us to be hopeful, knowing we are walking in life eternal. Won't you lay down whatever is keeping you bound and let hope begin to work in you today?

You can touch the throne with prayer.

Psalm 32
The Joy of Forgiveness

Blessed is he whose transgression is forgiven,
  whose sin is covered.
Blessed is the man unto who the Lord imputeth
  not iniquity, and in whose spirit is no guile.
When I kept silence my bones waxed old through
  my roaring all the day long.
For day and night thy hand was heavy upon me;
  My moisture is turned into the drought of summer.
I acknowledged my sin unto thee, and mine iniquity
  have I not hid.
I said I will confess my transgressions unto the Lord;
  and thou forgavest the iniquity of my sin.
For this everyone that is Godly pray unto thee in
  a time when though mayest be found;
Surely the floods of great waters they shall not
  come nigh unto him.

CHAPTER TWENTY

Forgiveness, Your Road to Freedom

*But as for you, you meant evil against me; But
God meant it for good, in order to bring it about
as it is this day, To save many people alive.*
Genesis 50:20

Here I am going through another set of prison doors, I
thought to myself as the last one clanged shut behind me.
I had no idea what was waiting for me on the other side of
that silent gray wall but I did know I had come prepared for
anything.

I was still weak from the previous week's stay in the hospital and even though my body was in a weakened state I had
never been more keenly aware of the spiritual strength that
was literally flooding my very being. I knew there was no
turning back from this point and in fact I was eager to get on
with it.

The usual twenty-minute wait stretched my nerves so each

noise was magnified and exaggerated. It seemed to be taking forever for them to bring in the man who was the reason for all of this heightened emotion, my father.

It had been five years since I had seen him last and that had not been behind prison walls. It had also not been my choice. He was allowed to go to his mother's funeral and it had been a shock to see him there, still so strong and intimidating looking. I still had that image of him in my mind so the little girl inside of me was terrified that he would find fault with me and place expectations on me that I could not fulfill.

As the minutes dragged by I had an overwhelming urge to run from that gray room where every move you made was monitored by the guards in the room on the other side of the glass partition. Kent must have sensed I was beginning to panic because he reached over and took my hand and said if I wanted to leave we could.

There was nothing keeping us there and if it was too much to handle we would just leave. It was exactly the right thing to say and it calmed me in an instant. Just knowing I could leave was instant relief. No sooner had I calmed down than the door the guard had pointed out to us as the one he would come through opened and there he was, no longer intimidating and frightening, but the man who was my father. The father I had loved, feared, adored and always tried to please as a child was standing only ten feet away.

As soon as I saw him my heart melted toward him and love began to flood through me. He had changed so much and I knew just by observing him that his health was not very good. He was no longer the man who evoked fear just by being in the same room with me. He was one of God's hurting children that had not found his way home yet.

In one moment all of the hardness and anger I had stored for so many years literally melted away and they were being replaced with love, compassion, tenderness and a thousand other emotions that I could not give voice to. This all happened in 30 seconds! He still had not spoken and neither had we! My experience was completely with the Lord and I knew in an instant why I was there and who the miracle was for!

As I introduced my husband and child to my father that day, I knew it wouldn't really matter what happened during the rest of the visit. My chains had come off and I was free from the prison I had been in for the past 23 years.

Throughout the next three hours a boldness I had never experienced before, especially when talking to my father, began to flavor our conversation. Even though I knew what I had just experienced, my father did not have a clue so he continued to behave toward me as he always had, bullying me a bit and demanding to know why I had come to see him after 16 years. Of course, that was at the end of the visit because he barely spoke to me for the first two and a half hours!

As I answered him I was very clear in telling him I was there because the Lord had asked me to go and then I asked him if he had ever been saved or water baptized. He said no to both questions and I told him I would be praying for him and I hugged him good-bye. The last thing I said to him was "I love you, Daddy!" The guard came and took him through the same door he had entered.

As we went back through all the clanging gates I was overwhelmed by the visit and what God had done for me. It was a few minutes before I could pull myself together to explain to my husband what had happened. I began to see the whole experience through my spirit eyes and I began to understand that because of my unforgiveness I had caused my father to have a limited life and that bondage had also limited my own life.

Now, through THE HEALING POWER OF FORGIVENESS I

began to walk in abundant life. By taking this first step toward healing, my entire family could begin to walk in freedom. It was a powerful revelation from my heavenly Father. I knew in that moment I began to walk in a freedom in my relationship to my heavenly Father that I had never experienced before. As tears of release poured down my face we came to a sign that said, "Don't give up, prayer works." I knew that my heavenly Father was looking down and reassuring me that I never had to worry about calling Him Father again. He was equipping me for the times to come with the most powerful tools He, my heavenly Father could give to me, His child, THE POWER OF PRAYER and THE HEALING POWER OF FORGIVENESS!

Acts 10:34 tells us "...God is no respecter of persons." So, remember what He has done for me and my family, He will do for you and yours!

Don't give up, the healing power of
forgiveness WORKS!

Epilogue

As this book goes into print it has been three years (almost to the day) since I entered those stark prison walls. In the very beginning of this manuscript I tried to convey my purpose in writing this story.

From the very moment I made the decision to make the trip to see my father all of the things that were happening in my life began to turn around. We saw my father on October 15, 1993 for the first time in sixteen years. On October 22, 1993, we were notified of the cancellation of a debt to the IRS we could never have paid in the natural. My relationships began to be healed and at this time in my life, I have never been healthier. As soon as my emotions began to heal my colon started to function properly and as the poison of bitterness left my heart, so did the 30 pounds of waste that had been poisoning my body! I no longer experience migraine headaches and I am walking in the liberty that Christ died for me to have!

My desire is to see God's people blessed and walking in liberty. My intent is not to judge my father or to present him in a less than respectful light. I have deliberately stayed away from sensationalism and specific details that would distract from what God did in my life.

My father is still in prison. Our relationship has never been closer. We have both made many mistakes in our past and together we are working through the ones that have affected our father-daughter relationship.

When he reads this book I pray the Holy Spirit will continue the work that has begun in his life. There have been many changes in both our lives since October 15, 1993, but I know there are many more to come.

In the meantime, I will continue to love, minister to and support my father. When the time comes for him to receive Jesus Christ as his Lord and Savior it will be a divine appointment orchestrated by the Father Himself.

All of your prayers are very much appreciated. As I close I'd like to pray for you.

Dear Heavenly Father,

As Your people come to You for strength and guidance reveal Yourself to them. Strengthen them for the trials to come and increase their faith so they may finish the course You have set before them. Put forgiveness in their hearts so they may be effective witnesses for Your kingdom. Turn their hearts to You, lead them by Your precious Holy Spirit and increase their ability to trust You to change the impossible. Bless Your servants, Lord God Almighty.

In Jesus' name we pray, Amen.

Points to Remember

1. Know that you can't forgive on your own, it is only by God's grace.

2. Making the decision to forgive not only frees you but also releases the person who hurt you.

3. Walking in forgiveness must be done in faith.

4. If you can't forgive yourself you won't be able to forgive others.

5. When God gives the command to forgive, He also gives the forgiveness.

6. To overcome rejection, forgiveness must come.

7. As you forgive those who have hurt or abused or rejected you, begin to bless them.

8. Ask God to use the very hurts you have experienced to be a starting place for a deeper relationship with Him.

9. Realize that unforgiveness keeps you bound from knowing God's true plan for your life and limits you ability to see what could be accomplished if you would allow Him to move on your behalf.

10. Be prepared to battle spiritual wickedness in high places for the liberty and peace forgiveness brings, because there will come a wilderness time of testing and trials.

11. Pride is the root of division. Don't let pride prevent you from having a forgiving heart.

12. It is our nature to run from pain and hurt, but confronting pain allows us the freedom to forgive those who have hurt us.

13. Satan will use our weaknesses again and again to attack us.

14. Once we are aware there is unforgiveness in our lives we can open the door for healing to take place in our own lives.

15. When you are unable to forgive, you are bound by judgment.

16. Unforgiveness keeps you bound by someone else's actions.

17. To walk in forgiveness, the love of Christ must be extended.

18. Forgiveness is a deliberate choice to be obedient to God who forgave us all our sins through the blood of Jesus Christ of Nazareth.

19. Even though unforgiveness may not be a deliberate decision to disobey God, it still prevents God from accomplishing His perfect will in us.

20. Forgiveness will bring peace into your hearts.

21. When you make the choice to forgive it doesn't mean the hurts didn't occur. It does mean you are submitted to Christ and you are trusting Him to help you walk in forgiveness.

22. The act of forgiveness not only frees the person that has harmed you, but also removes any stumbling blocks in your relationship with your heavenly Father.

23. The bitterness that comes with an unforgiving heart ultimately affects every area of your life.

24. When we don't accept the forgiveness that was given to us by Christ dying on the cross, we hinder our entire relationship with God.

25. When we can't or won't accept God's gift of forgiveness, we can't accept His unconditional love and His mercy and grace.

26. You are uniquely created in God's image.

27. You are forgiven for not being perfect.

28. You are still in the process of growing and changing.

29. You are what God has made you.

30. Forgiveness is a way of life.

31. We can't change our past but we can change our reaction to it.

32. By making the choice to obey God's Word, we as children of the most high, Living God, our heavenly Father, have a glorious future!